★SMOKY★
★SWEATY★
★ROWDY★
AND
★LOUD★

Also by Mike & Janice Olszewski

Cleveland Radio Tales
Cleveland TV Tales
Cleveland TV Tales, Volume 2

SMOKY SWEATY ROWDY *and* LOUD

TALES OF

CLEVELAND'S LEGENDARY ROCK & ROLL LANDMARKS

MIKE & JANICE OLSZEWSKI

GRAY & COMPANY, PUBLISHERS

CLEVELAND

Gray & Company, Publishers
www.grayco.com

ISBN: 978-1-59851-104-8
Printed in the U.S.A.

1

To Irv Fine, Linn Sheldon, and Bob West, three men whom we were honored to count among our dearest friends. Their legacy lives on.

Contents

Introduction

THERE IS NO REAL argument about Cleveland's role in rock and roll history. This city must have led the nation in breaking national acts, great radio (yeah, we're a bit biased), and records bought, per capita, by the public.

And there's no doubt about rock's role in Cleveland history, either. Rock and roll held Cleveland together when many thought the city was circling the drain.

Cleveland was still considered a big city into the mid-1960s, but by 1970 many factors had led to a near-meltdown. During the '70s and for quite some time after, the only reasons to go downtown were a job, to catch the Indians or the Browns, or to see a great rock show by a well-known artist or a new band looking to break out. Credit for the last goes to radio, a rapidly evolving medium led by local visionaries who understood the power of the audience and the influence it had in reshaping Greater Cleveland. The music our parents considered a dangerous fad (at best) wound up playing a significant role in making Cleveland a better place to live.

Great rock and roll has been made in garages and bars, huge arenas and public parks. Northeast Ohio has had some of the best of those. This book covers notable venues in Cleveland's rock and roll history, from dive bars like the Euclid Tavern to cavernous Cleveland Municipal Stadium.

The stories of those venues pivot on colorful characters, the people who made the places come alive before a single note was played: the raconteurs, barflies, and avid music lovers who came to the shows became part of local pop culture history.

We've tried to feature as many places and people as possible. But could we cover them all? No. Northeast Ohio's history is too rich for one book of this size. We know people will ask, "Why didn't you include the Odeon or Peabody's or Blossom?" Or "What about the Circle Theater, the Versailles Motor Inn, the Dove Lounge . . . ?"

OK, so tell us . . .

Did you see Glass Harp at Southgate or the James Gang at Parmatown when they opened the Way-In Shops at the May Company stores in those malls? How about Frankenstein at the Viking Saloon, the Cleveland State bar—before they evolved into the Dead Boys? T. Rex at Parma's Yorktown Theatre? Maybe you were at the mudfest when Deep Purple played Cloverleaf Speedway. You might have caught Bell Telefunk (sometimes spelled "Telephunk") at Sir-Rah House before the band changed its name and later topped charts as Dazz Band.

Elton John at Kent State? Pink Floyd at Case Western Reserve University's Emerson Gym? Maybe you saw King Crimson play the Peaches record store in Maple Heights. The Alarm Clocks, now in regular rotation on Sirius XM's "Underground Garage," played out of a real garage in Parma. Damnation of Adam Blessing had a residency at D'Poos Tool & Die Works in the Flats. A handful of people saw Jimi Hendrix wander into Otto's Grotto to play with the band Good Earth after his shows at Music Hall.

All those shows were long ago, and we've lost many of those favorite spots over the years. But the memories we can keep alive. This book is a first step.

(You can help us take the *next* step—by getting in touch and sharing your memories, photos, and memorabilia for a second book. Send us an email in care of: editorial@grayco.com.)

Let's dig into our first batch of stories. Slip on some patched jeans, fill up that old wine sack, and as John Lennon once sang, "Turn off your mind, relax, and float downstream." Let's revisit an era when great music thundered from small clubs and huge arenas alike, for the same reason: peace, love, and rock and roll—or any combination of the three.

The Cleveland Arena

3717 Euclid Avenue, Cleveland

WHEN THE YOUTH CULTURE first reared its head after World War II, you saw the first baby steps of the upcoming generation gap that would define American culture by the 1960s. Many elements helped define the first years of rock and roll in the late 1940s and early '50s. Televisions started to pop up in homes across America, and young people with part-time jobs, discretionary cash, and cars weren't satisfied to sit around the house with mom and dad, staring at a screen, for long. The golden age of radio was coming to a quick end as many of its stars moved to the new medium. Kids developed their own fashions, entertainment, and even language. Radio stations found it cheaper to play records than pay live musicians, and the disc jockey was born.

Folks born in the first half of the 20th century looked for something to unite the country after making it through World War II. They controlled the media, which always seemed to report new dangers threatening the American way of life. Senator Joe McCarthy and his henchman Roy Cohn warned of a communist plot to take over the U.S. like some sort of Soviet manifest destiny. Dr. Fredric Wertham linked comic books to juvenile delinquency. UFOs were said to threaten our airspace.

In a country deeply divided by race, there was no greater threat than black artists making music for white kids. The devil's music was coming right into your son's or daughter's bedroom, Satan's voice blasting loud and clear every night on WJW radio. And in this scenario, the portal to hell was the Cleveland Arena.

Alan Freed was the visionary with the drive, the smarts, and the pipes to sell black music to a white audience. What he was not was an overnight success. He grew up in Salem, Ohio, and wanted a career in music. At Ohio State University, Freed became interested in radio, a highly competitive field at the time. After leaving the Army, Freed paid his dues at radio stations in New Castle, Pennsylvania, and Youngstown, getting his big break at Akron's WAKR. Freed wore a lot of hats at that AM station (FM wasn't around yet), playing music, reporting sports, and hosting dances for extra cash.

Freed liked playing rhythm and blues by the original artists, and folks in Akron liked what he was doing. But he still struggled. He called football games, did a classical show, and even started a broadcasting school that shut down in a year after no one signed on. (Let's be practical here. Why sign up for a course that would send you to a postage stamp of a station for a few years to get your chops when there were plenty of good-paying jobs right out of high school in Akron's rubber industry?) He became acquainted with Leo Mintz, owner of Cleveland's Record Rendezvous, who offered to sponsor a show on WJW if Freed pushed the so-called "race" records available in Mintz's store.

Here's the way Leo's son, Stu, recalls it.

"In the early '50s, Alan was working with a station out of Akron (WAKR) and he knew he couldn't go anywhere. He met my dad, and he said at the time he could bring him to Cleveland and get him a job on WJW, which at that time was into black music. He eventually got Alan on the all-night show and gave him the name Moondog, and that ran for a few years. Alan probably had one of the biggest followings in the country."

There were no racial barriers at Record Rendezvous. Stu will tell you, "In those days it was before the shopping centers. Everybody in the city came downtown to shop. Since we had the biggest record inventory in the city, we got almost primarily all the business." But even then, labeling something with race could be a divisive issue. Stu says his dad saw that music helped level the playing field. "During that time customers who came to Record Rendezvous could play their own records. They had record players they

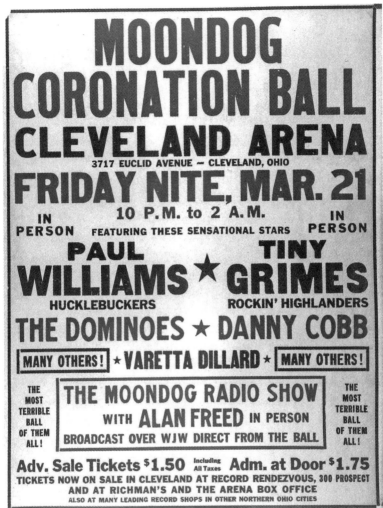

The most terrible ball of them all! Alan Freed's plan to be crowned "King of the Moondoggers" came to an abrupt end when the overflow crowd stormed the Arena's doors. *(Courtesy of Janet Macoska)*

could play records on. He noticed that white kids were coming down and listening to race music, which was black music at that time, but they wouldn't buy it because it was race music. He knew he needed a name for the kids from the Heights to buy it. He was talking to Alan and he said, 'The kids come in rocking and they roll all day long! They listen to the music but they won't buy it. We gotta do something.' That was how it started. Plain and simple." A few simple words that would shake the world.

Stu also recalls Leo Mintz selling the term to Freed. "My dad was a very animated person. As he was talking to Alan he was telling him, 'They rock. They roll. Use it!' Alan got on the air and said, 'Okay, c'mon kids! You're gonna rock and roll at the Rendez-vous!' It took off right from there." Like a missile, though it took some haggling to get Freed off the launch pad.

The demand was obviously there. Pretty soon for Freed it was "So long, Akron!" Time to move on to bigger and better things. But there was one big problem: Freed had signed a non-compete contract with WAKR so he couldn't work on radio elsewhere for a few months, while WAKR hoped that folks would forget him in that time. Still, Freed had a family and needed cash flow. Television was just starting out, and Freed took a gig as a staff announcer and as host of an afternoon movie at Cleveland's WXEL, Channel 9, which paid next to nothing. Freed was used to a radio paycheck and Leo Mintz helped him out a lot, but for extra cash he also tended bar at the Kent Hotel near Kent State University. Today, some of the great names in popular music play the Kent Stage with no idea that the guy who helped define rock and roll once drew beer across the street.

Freed finally opened the mic at WJW in July 1951 to host a classical music show, but it wasn't long before he was playing rhythm and blues. Between Mintz and the Standard Brewing Company's Erin Brew, he was making pretty good coin. Word got around about his show, too, and 850 AM shortly became the go-to spot on the dial at night. The show was bigger than your little radio speaker, and seven months after his arrival Freed decided to push live shows. Seemed like a great idea. Even so, there were dark clouds on the horizon.

Even though Leo Mintz reportedly told Freed "the kids are rocking and rolling in the aisles of his store" on East Fourth and Prospect, at first Freed called it "moondog music." After all, this was the "Moondog Show" on WJW. Freed, Mintz, Akron concert promoter Lew Platt, and an investor named Milton Kulkin decided to stage a "Moondog Coronation Ball" at the Cleveland Arena on March 21, 1952, with each act building to the point where Freed would be crowned "King of the Moondoggers," along with the winners of a teenage popularity contest. Platt wasn't Mintz's first choice to promote the concert. Another dance promoter, Booker Brooks, had promoted similar shows with Freed in Akron and Canton, and was working with him to present Count Basie and his orchestra at the Arena. Basie canceled, Brooks was out, and Platt was brought in to book other acts for the show.

It should be stressed that this was not the first of the so-called "balls." Stu tells us, "It was the Moondog Ball brought to you by Record Rendezvous. My dad helped produce it and brought the artists in. Most people know it as the Moondog Ball at the Arena. It was a series, and every weekend they would have a ball somewhere. They had them at Euclid Beach amusement park; a park out of Akron; McKinley Heights near Girard, Ohio—they had them all over. It was like every weekend in the summer. They were bringing hundreds and hundreds of kids. Alan would always emcee it . . . and then they had 'the most terrible ball of them all.' That pretty much put an end to all of them. That was really the first great rock concert of the time. All black artists, of course."

It really was billed as "the most terrible ball of them all," and in hindsight Freed might have wanted to reword that. Word got around, too. Shirlee Bryant wrote in her "East Hi-Lites" column in the *Call & Post* that "everyone's talking about the coming Moondog dance, March 21 at the Arena. From what I hear, it's going to be a dance that everyone remembers." Boy, would they!

The lineup that night included Paul Williams and the Huckle-

buckers, who had a hit called "The Hucklebuck." There was also
Tiny Grimes and his Rockin' Highlanders (a black R&B group
that wore kilts as stage costumes), Danny Cobb, the Dominoes,
and Varetta Dillard. This wasn't a show for the early birds. It was
scheduled to start at 10 p.m. and run until 2 the next morning.
Tickets went fast, too—6,000 advanced sale—and they weren't
cheap for the time at $1.75 a head, but that was a lot of entertain-
ment, with Alan Freed to boot. The audience should have had seat
belts for the ride they were about to take.

That Friday night the stage was set, the acts were in their dressing rooms, and Freed was ready to greet the masses. People came
from Toledo, Akron, Lorain, and all points in between. Lots of
people, way more than expected, and it didn't end there. At first
glance everything looked well in hand. Leo Mintz left his brother-
in-law, Milt Kulkin, the guy Freed called "Uncle Miltie," in charge.

This was going to be a big night. Before the show Freed and his
wife were enjoying steaks in his dressing room while the acts got
ready to take the stage. Kulkin looked out the window and did a
double take. There were long lines of people down Euclid Avenue,
waiting to get into the show. Really long lines. Fingers were crossed
that everyone would enter the hall in an orderly manner. Turns
out crossed fingers weren't enough. This Titanic, too, was heading
for an iceberg.

Stu Mintz remembers that day well. "The only place you could
buy tickets were at Richman Brothers clothing stores or my dad's
store. They sold out in one day, 7,500 tickets. So my dad said, 'Okay.
Done! It's Stu's birthday. Let's all go to Florida.' I remember on the
airplane my dad had the stewardesses make a birthday party for
me. It was my seventh birthday. We got to Florida and my dad gets
a call. 'Leo! Come home!' This was the day of the concert. He takes
a plane back to Cleveland and he sees the riot going on."

Turns out there was a slight mistake on some of the tickets.
Okay, maybe it was a really big mistake.

As Stu remembers, "What happened was Uncle Miltie said,
'Well, we sold the tickets that fast, I'm going to have another show

and have 7,500 more tickets printed up!' Well, they printed the tickets . . . for the same show! Fifteen thousand people showed up, and they were breaking windows, the cops brought the fire hoses out, and it could have been one of the first race riots in the country."

Leo Mintz arrived just in time to witness the mayhem.

"In those days it was like a five- to six-hour ride in a Lockheed Constellation plane with propellers. He took a taxi from the airport straight to the Arena, saw what was going on, and didn't bother to get out. He just left." Back to Florida. What a night!

Mob rule gets real ugly real quick, and that night was a prime example. No one is really sure exactly how many people were denied entry, but a safe bet is it was in the thousands. Initial reports in the *Plain Dealer* put the number at 6,000 pushing down the doors, adding to another 14,000 inside, which seems exaggerated for a hall that had a maximum capacity far less than that—about 10,000 to 11,000. One thing for sure is that the police had their hands full and it wasn't going to get any better. The paper called it a "confined mass of humanity," and the crowd kept getting bigger and angrier when people were denied entry. The crowd surged, knocked down four Arena doors and pushed cops aside to make their way into the hall. Police radioed for backup, and 30 more cops raced to the scene. There was no way to restore order. A Cleveland Police captain named Zimmerman halted the show. That didn't make the crowd any happier.

Fights broke out, with punches flying, hair pulling, people shoving, and one guy getting his eye gouged. Now, here's the irony. Freed was promoting a concert of black music for both white and black kids. Mainstream newspapers like the *Cleveland Press*, the *Cleveland News*, and the *Plain Dealer* reported the melee, but there was a lot of other news. The *PD* ran the story as a small article on page one but well below the fold, and it got relatively little coverage after that. It was the city's paper for the black community, the *Call & Post*, that was outraged, and columnist Valena Minor Williams tore Freed a new one. Williams was at the show and estimated the crowd size at 20,000. She called it an instance of mass hysteria that couldn't be explained or controlled. She said the trouble started at 9:15, 45 minutes before the show, with a dispute over the availability of tickets at the box office. Williams called that show's lineup "a galaxy of not quite famous recording artists whose weird rhythms have been the substance" of Freed's nightly show. She correctly stated that Freed was playing "lesser known Negro recording artists whose waxings seldom appear on other programs—not even those manned by Negro disc jockeys." Williams said Freed's show targeted teenagers and, by her estimates, less than one percent of the crowd that night was white. But here's where Williams touches on the real problem. Freed announced on his show the night before that the initial run of tickets had sold out and 2,000 more were being printed. They would be available at noon the Friday of the show. She said there was something about the crowd that terrified her, and when she told that to Lew Platt he let out a laugh. He wouldn't have much to laugh about after that.

Police shut down the bar (always a popular move for an angry crowd!), and Williams saw shattered glass and hoped the door she was behind would hold. She called out to one cop, "I wouldn't want to be a policeman for anything on a night like this," and he shouted back, "I don't think I want to be after this!" Williams made her way to the door and was somehow able to hail a cab, but the crowds kept coming, stopping traffic. The taxi slowly made its way to East 46th Street before it could go at normal speed. When Williams walked through her door she turned on the radio and found, not surprisingly, that WJW had cut the live broadcast from the Arena. The photographer she was working with said five fire trucks rolled up after she left.

Williams said she was shocked that Freed's show appealed to so many black teenagers and that their parents tolerated it. She said the "gut bucket blues and low-down rhythms" were an addiction that compelled the kids to rush the Arena. Williams ended by saying Freed exploited "Negro teensters," and called for action by the community. Williams wasn't alone. That same paper editorialized that Freed was a "fast talking, wise cracking Pied Piper" who

How did that happen? No one anticipated just how people would react when they were told the Arena was filled to capacity. Plenty of broken windows would tell that story.
(Cleveland Press Collection, Cleveland State University Archives)

lit a fire under 20,000 blues fans (again a new number) to "provide the populace with an unparalleled example of bad manners, teenage vice and bold disdain" for their parents and police. The unnamed writer said a near-riot was averted by the "quick action of Negro policemen in the crowd, familiar with the lawless element that had infiltrated the group," and said their efforts helped avoid "a disastrous blow to future race relations in Cleveland." But it wasn't just the bad apples in the crowd. The paper took aim at Freed and the promoters saying, "There is certainly sufficient evidence that they 'oversold' their house to dangerous proportions, and that they lacked both the courage and foresight to handle the inescapable result." Ouch!

Finally, another shot over the bow. The paper said "responsibility lies in the laps of parents of the several thousand teenagers, most of whom should have been in bed long before the police" were called in. The writer took a stand, saying Freed and his partners should have recognized the potential danger at earlier shows in Akron and Canton, calling the promoter "unscrupulous," and saying the event was loaded with "teen-age dynamite!" Like that's a bad thing! The article said juvenile delinquents poured into the show "wearing their hats inside a public place, guzzling liquor without restraint from pocket flasks and, here and there, actually shooting themselves with narcotics in the midst of the crowd!" Well, not the entire crowd. The author suggested that hundreds who attended showed good manners and wore nice clothes, but they didn't realize Freed's show wasn't going to help. After all, what do you wear to a riot? The show was called the "foundation of immorality, vulgar suggestion and hidden indecency." If rock and roll needed a bad reputation, this author was adding to it quickly, and there was more. It went on about a "weed smoking element" that put up a "loud and vulgar clamor" that drowned out the performers onstage. The paper called for a ticket refund, legal action, and the "moondog madness" to come to an end. The legal action was the most distinct possibility.

The next morning, Assistant Fire Captain Emmett Porter and Assistant Police Prosecutor Bernard Conway met to discuss possible charges against Freed and his crew, but they weren't sure if they could prove any violation was intentional. The real danger manifested in the court of public opinion, which made Freed nervous. Big time! The very next night a more subdued Freed cracked the microphone to give an emotional apology. At times he seemed close to tears, and he stressed that while he had great respect for promoter Lew Platt, he was only an employee that night, not a co-promoter. Out in radio land promoter Booker Brooks said that was "bull," claiming it was Freed who called the shots when he couldn't produce Count Basie for the show.

The apology was called one of the most unusual in the history of radio, and Freed admitted the newspapers wanted him in jail. Overcrowding? Not as he saw it. Freed claimed the Internal Revenue Service put ticket sales at 9,700, fewer than the 13,000 the Harlem Globetrotters drew a few weeks before, though a newspaper report said Freed cited 10,000 fans outside the hall and 7,000 didn't have tickets. Would he step down? Freed was a pretty savvy promoter. He said, "Let's leave it to the listeners." If you want me out, say so, he urged. He said there had been speculation that he would skip town, and he thanked the WJW management for their "understanding." (Listeners also heard a lot of commercials for Erin Brew beer and other spots. They understood, all right.)

The calls poured in and—surprise!—they supported Freed. To show his thanks, he promised a new and better concert with free admission to folks with Moondog Ball tickets. He also admitted the show would likely have to be out in the country to accommodate the crowds. A bullet was dodged, but the legal problems were far from over. A woman who had attended the Moondog Ball filed a lawsuit claiming she was pushed down the steps at the Arena and trampled by the mob. She sought $7,500 in damages in a personal injury suit for "bruises and contusions." Her attorneys said the Arena comfortably fit 7,000 for a dance, but 25,000 showed up, smashing windows, and causing a near-riot.

The *Call & Post* wasn't done with Freed either. In a series of articles titled, "Today's Youngsters: Teen-Agers or Moon-Doggers?," staff writer Marty Richardson cited an "epidemic of low-brow, cheap entertainment" on radio. He called it "frequently obscene and generally in poor taste," describing Freed's "Moon-Dog Howl" as a "masterpiece of lyric garbage." Freed's show ran from 11 p.m. to 2 a.m. with an afternoon matinee thrown in. Richardson admitted that he liked a lot of stuff Freed played, but said the Moon-Dog concept was a "wholesale perversion of the love of young people for music into an appreciation of, and exposure to, the lowest, most vulgar, most insulting type of 'entertainment' that greedy recording companies could put onto wax and stay out of jail." What kid reading this would not want the forbidden fruit? There's more, and he came out with both guns blazing. He cited records by Piney Brown, H-Bomb Ferguson and the Hambone Kids, and T-Bone Walker, the same people Freed said would appear at future Moon-Dog dances! Richardson warned all purgatory would break loose, drawing marijuana smokers, wine heads, pickpockets, and car robbers, not to mention "a lot of men and women who carry shiny little needles in their pockets" to shoot heroin if the show got boring. There would be "pimps and prostitutes and robbers and dope fiends" mingling with students from Central High and John Hay. He warned about problems like one seen at the Cleveland Arena in which seven girls beat up one of their boyfriends in front of the stage among "wine bottles that littered the floor" and "several people who openly jabbed dope into their arms on the dance floor."

Richardson preached against obscenity and filth on the airwaves that appealed to ages from 60 down to 6. But hold it; not so fast. An East High student wrote to say that Freed played that music because there was a demand for it, and record companies produced it for that same reason. Richardson countered, arguing that songs like "Dancing My Fannie Around," "My Daddy Rocks Me," and "Long Tall Papa" were not an automatic response to people's tastes but ran to "hogwash." He blamed little "hole in the wall record companies" as well as "million dollar corporations" and "studio-in-the-attic-operators who still owe payments on $200 worth of equipment they finally got together." He didn't blame racism, saying "There are colored companies and white companies turning out records every day to swell the estimated $10,000,000 worth of them that are made annually. There are people of every racial, religious and moral stratum in the business." But he did say there were people "turning out the trash that attracts the lowest elements like moths around a bright glowing light, that attract the sane, sensible young seekers after genuine entertainment in the same orbit." Does this sound like the movie "Reefer Madness" or what?

In the coming weeks, Richardson would credit fine youngsters for the avalanche of letters defending Freed and other "purveyors

The Cleveland Arena, the city's second-biggest performance venue of its day, was mostly known for sporting events and family fare until rock and rollers moved in and shook the roof. *(Cleveland Press Collection, Cleveland State University Archives)*

of recorded filth." We sense just a hint of bias. They were "well written, reasonable and sincere" even though they defended the man who brought "indecent, vulgar, obscene, low-brow gut-bucket music" to a keenly appreciative public. He applauded efforts for stricter laws to restrict crowd size, but also played the race card. Richardson now stated there was not a "single Negro distributor of records in the land" despite the fact that black people were the largest consumers per capita of records in the world. He also took aim at white record executives, asking whether they produced the same type of material for Irish, Hungarian or Jewish consumers as for folks who bought "race" records. He said many of those records were so dirty "they wouldn't pass a deaf, dumb and blind board of censors." He also asked if "there are three Negro orchestras in the whole country making money today since the 'Moon-Dog' vogue of dirt-instead-of-music" had become the order of the day.

He also suggested asking Freed how many shows he promoted in Shaker Heights or Brook Park or "anywhere else where the attendance would have been anything other than colored." Crazy thought. How many of those cities had big arenas? Did the tickets say "blacks only"?

Yet still Richardson wasn't done. A few days later in that same paper he cited a "vicious circle of exploitation of listeners and public alike; an exploitation that has YOU as victim." Richardson blamed record promoters for not giving black artists better songs to sing. Why did Rosemary Clooney and Frank Sinatra get songs like "With a Song in My Heart" instead of "Rock Little Daddy"? He said it was because there was not "a single large company owned by Negroes making records in the whole country." Richardson went on to say, "except for a few guys who distribute a handful of records for use in their own juke-boxes, there is not a single Negro distributor of records in the land." Then the bombshell. "A Race record is a Jim Crow record!"

Richardson wouldn't let up, making Freed and the event at the Cleveland Arena a platform for fanning the flames: "These unscrupulous Merchants of Filth give the composers of the trash no protection whatsoever for their labor." What's more, he charged, "the company owns the 'master' records, they often keep no books or keep crooked books, and the artist never knows what royalties are due him. It gets so bad that there is a band in Cleveland right now which recorded a smash-hit and never got a dime. When the recorder saw that he was about to make a pile of dough, he simply went out of business, 'sold' the master record to himself under another name, and the band was out of luck."

Okay, there is some merit to that argument, but white artists got hurt, too. Allen Klein may get a lot of bad press, but he made his name securing back royalties owed to artists like Sam Cooke. He had plenty to work with, too.

Richardson also predicted radio station managers were hearing his complaints, saying, "the popularization of uncensored obscenity produced and distributed by people whose only interest is the exploitation of every possible dime out of Negro pockets they can take" would soon come to an end. The Cleveland Arena clearly started a firestorm, and more letters came in ... but they defended Alan Freed!

One reader wrote, "Your articles not only seem to have bad facts, but show signs of prejudice and pride." An attorney wrote, "Tell us the whole story, and in passing out blame lay the major parts on the delinquent parents who abandon their children, their most precious possessions to drag in filth and fail to show them, for example, how glorious is the opera."

Granted, that may have been a stretch, but still another defended Freed, saying, "The Moon-Dog can't exploit a person unless he wants to be exploited. You have a narrow and prejudiced view." Seriously, how much criticism would have been generated without the Moondog Coronation Ball?

One person wrote, "I went to the Moon-Dog Ball and I agree a lot of damage was done. I hope Allen [sic] Freed keeps the good work up."

To the paper's credit, it published both sides, with one reader on Beulah Avenue writing that "by promoting songs that glorify the loud-mouthed, wine-drinking, knife-carrying, reefer-smoking type of person, certain disc jockeys have developed in the minds of our young people a kind of respect and adoration for these anti-so-cial characters." Another wrote, "I am writing on behalf of a group of teenagers on the East Side. I would like to prove that all teenag-ers are NOT turning into Moon-Doggers. We think it is unjust to accuse all teenagers of being 'drips' because we fell for the line of Allen [sic] Freed, and we would like a chance to defend ourselves."

Less than two months after the Moondog Coronation Ball, Freed and his friends decided to try it all over again at the same place. They obviously didn't want a repeat of the problems in the first show, so they booked the Arena for two days and three shows on May 17 and 18. That included a teenage matinee on Sunday the 18th.

The Arena management didn't want any problems, so it took over promotion and ticket sales. The "Moondog Maytime Festi-val" promised an "array of bands and vaudeville acts," with the

Dominoes, Freddie Mitchell of "Moondog Boogie" fame, H-Bomb Ferguson, Jackie Brenston, Fats Thomas and a slew of other acts. Little Jimmy Scott, a native Clevelander with a high, eerie voice, was on the bill, too. A unique talent whose distinctive vocals were the result of a hereditary condition known as Kallmann syndrome, Scott never reached puberty but had a singing career with Lionel Hampton and several other bands. He made several major-label recordings, toured with Lou Reed and appeared in director David Lynch's TV series "Twin Peaks." Scott died in 2014.

Fingers were crossed that no problems would occur this time. Shirlee Bryant urged Moondoggers in her "East Hi-Lites" column in the *Call & Post* to "leave the bottles, profane language, and all the weapons at home. And let's prove to all the people who think all 'Moondoggers' are hoodlums and addicts that they are wrong, that we're just fun-loving teenagers who are judged by a few bad kids."

The police didn't want problems either. On the night of the first show there were 52 extra cops on hand, including eight mounted police, another 29 on call, and a fire department detail. When the show started at 10 p.m., only about 25 percent of the 4,500 ticket holders were on hand, but by all accounts they saw a great concert.

The breakout star was Chess Records' Jackie Brenston, who tore the roof off the place leading his Rocket 88 orchestra with his wailing tenor sax. After the last act left the stage for the final show you heard a collective "Whew!" from the front office.

Freed decided to take the show back on the road, planning June stops for his "Moondog Moonlight Ball" in Lorain, Vermilion, Girard, and Akron. He even booked "modern, up to date busses" to ship fans in from Cleveland and back. Not all the moondog news was positive. A year later, a couple of inner-city kids were accused of armed robbery for allegedly sticking up four people after the Akron show. The papers called them, you guessed it, the "Moondog robbers."

On August 15, 1954, Freed signed off at WJW for the final time to head east to New York City and serious money: $75,000 a year. WJW promised to keep staging the Moondog shows in his memory. Freed even hosted a final concert, this one at Public Hall, the week before he left along with his "Mrs. Moondog and the Moon Puppies." The station hired "Moondog" Brinnon for the Circle Theater concert, and WSRS-FM's Sam "Crazy Man Crazy" Sampson booked a show of his own back at the Arena. They just didn't have the same fire.

Sampson blamed that very first Moondog show for continuing problems and claimed he was being persecuted for "sins he had not committed" and for city officials holding up his permit. The week before the concert Mayor Anthony Celebrezze said he'd had it with shows and dances of that type, but later gave the go-ahead to hold the concert—with no dancing. That hurt the box office, and the police paddy wagon and ambulance parked out front didn't help. The one bright spot came when WJW hired "Crazy Man Crazy" Sampson to take up Freed's banner. The original "King of the Moondoggers" went on to nationwide road shows, movies, and infamy on any number of levels.

So who was the "big dog" tearing up the record charts in the mid-'50s? A lot of rock and rollers were getting their share of attention; name the act and the kids were dancing to it, but Elvis Presley was in a class all by himself.

Did Presley ever play the Arena? Yeah, he did, but he needed some help. The disc jockeys at WERE saw Presley's potential but in a different way. Tommy Edwards had a "hillbilly music" show and saw Presley as a country act. At the same time, Bill Randle liked Presley as a rock and roller. Both jocks got a chance to test their theories.

On October 19, 1955, Edwards placed Presley third on the bill at one of his "Hillbilly Hayride" shows at the Circle Theater on East 105th Street. Presley opened for Kitty Wells and Faron Young, and when he walked off the stage he sat at a card table in the lobby. Alone. Few stopped by to say hello, but the next day would go down in history.

Randle hosted a five-act show at Brooklyn High School on Cleveland's west side. You had the Four Lads, Priscilla Wright, Bill

Haley and the Comets, and the headliner, Pat Boone. Presley was the third act up, and this one was for the rock and rollers. Filmed for a short about Randle called *The Pied Piper of Cleveland*, it purportedly shows Presley doing his first rock and roll show north of the Mason–Dixon line. The film has been missing for years, but that's another mystery to solve.

Later that night, Randle took that same lineup to a dance at the St. Mary's CYO Hall at East 100th Street and Union Avenue, where Presley smashed a guitar on stage. So how did he go from playing dances to the Arena just a year later? Television and a brand-new record contract helped.

Two months after those shows, RCA bought Presley's contract from Sam Phillips at Sun Records. In January 1956, Randle introduced Presley to a nationwide TV audience on the *Dorsey Brothers Stage Show*. In the coming months he scored five number one hits, put out one record after another including "Heartbreak Hotel" and "Blue Suede Shoes," and released his first film, *Love Me Tender*. The Arena date was set for November 23rd.

There was a newspaper strike, so what we know about that show comes from the few people still around today who saw it. Fortunately, 17-year old Lew Allen was covering the concert for *The Black and Gold*—the Cleveland Heights High School newspaper. The kid was a really good photographer. The year before, Allen had won a prestigious award at Kent State University with a program aimed at teaching young journalists how to cover breaking news. He remembers well the call that changed his life.

"I was in our yearbook room at the school and my advisor got the call from Elvis's label, RCA," Allen says. "The PR guy said he needed a reporter and photographer to cover the show. All three Cleveland newspapers were on strike, but Heights High had a reputation for a great journalism program."

Turns out it was the right place, right time . . . and what a time!

"We didn't have a car," Allen continues, "so the reporter, Carol Specter, and I loaded my lights and camera on the bus. Those were the days when you dressed up for events like this. We got to the

Arena and knocked on the back door. 'Newspaper people are here!' They gave us press passes, and even though it was our first big assignment they gave us full access everywhere. 'Do what you like. Take as many shots as you want.' Then it kicked into high gear.

"Elvis walked in wearing a trench coat, with some Cleveland police as body guards. Remember the actor Nick Adams? He was a friend of James Dean and Natalie Wood—he was there, too."

Presley knew why Allen and Specter were there, and he was happy to work with them. Allen described Presley as very down-to-earth, modest, and extremely polite.

"I was snapping pictures and there were a few casual conversations. The PR guy for RCA had two girls pose side by side with Elvis, and I said, 'No! You should kiss him!' and they did. Then I called out, 'Hey Elvis!' and he gave me the weirdest stare, just for the camera. Great shot!"

On top of that, Presley heard of a fan who wanted to be at the show but was in the hospital. He called her and spent about 15 minutes chatting before he had to hit the stage. In fact, the show started late because of that call, but when Elvis took the stage it was like nothing Allen had ever seen.

"Thousands of maniacal screaming girls, and most of the audience were girls," Allen says. "It was thunderous, constant shrieking, and then they started rushing the stage! There was no way they could get on. It was six feet above the floor, and they had to get past the cops lined up in front. The police bounced them off their bellies and the girls landed on their asses! The cops were laughing!"

When you talk about Elvis in Cleveland, the name Bill Randle will always come up. Allen doesn't remember seeing him at the concert, but he might even have emceed the show. Randle heard about the photos and asked for enlargements. Allen was happy to comply and got 50 Erroll Garner records in exchange.

Allen's photos sat in storage for years until he was encouraged to have them issued as a high-end coffee table book by a noted British publisher. That limited-edition book is a hotly sought after collector's item today. The BBC even sent over a film crew to do a story.

Enter the King! Elvis Presley's show at the Cleveland Arena came during a newspaper strike. A teenage photographer for a high school newspaper captured the historic moment when Elvis entered the building. *(Lew Allen)*

The Cleveland Arena was never meant to be a concert hall. It was built for rodeos, and rasslin', and roller derby, with an occasional ice show or circus thrown in. The acoustics were horrible. But who came to a concert to hear the music? The Rolling Stones wished people had done that when they performed a matinee with the McCoys and the Standells at the Arena in June 1966.

The band was double-booked that Saturday, with an evening show in Pittsburgh. Jane Scott reviewed the Arena show in the *Plain Dealer*, saying Mick Jagger jumped around the stage like a "hopped up Indian." Maybe it was a weird show of appreciation, maybe just a call back to the Moondog show, but whatever it was, it was messy. Six thousand people showed up for the show and started showering the band with empty cups and crumpled popcorn bags, flash bulbs, anything that could be thrown. This was a difficult show for the Stones because they even had to scramble for hair dryers before they went onstage. There was plenty of security, but as the band finished the show and headed offstage the crowd surged ahead, pushing police aside. Some fans grabbed the Stones as they ran to the door. The Stones wouldn't return to Cleveland for a very long time.

The Arena would host the occasional concert, usually acts that couldn't draw at the better-known venues. But a concert in April 1972 may have been the last hurrah for that facility. A fund-raiser for Democratic presidential hopeful George McGovern, the show was a sellout, featuring star power Cleveland hadn't seen in years. More than 11,000 fans came out to see Paul Simon, in only his second solo appearance, James Taylor, and Joni Mitchell. Jane Scott likened Mitchell's voice to a "sophisticated yodel." Mitchell demanded silence during her performance, even from the ushers. That was a tall order because these celebrity ushers included Warren Beatty, Jack Nicholson, and Julie Christie, among others. After the show, the stars headed to the Diplomat Restaurant on East 31st and Euclid Avenue for a post-concert cocktail party with McGovern and Senator Ted Kennedy.

By 1974 the Cleveland Arena was 37 years old and seriously

looking its age. You had a hard time finding a parking space, the neighborhood didn't feel safe, and the then-brand-new Richfield Coliseum stole away the Cleveland Cavaliers and other events. It was time to fold the tent, and the building sat empty until 1977, when it met "the most terrible ball of them all," the wrecking ball, which brought the walls down on a lot of local history. On the site of the Arena now sits the headquarters for the Cleveland chapter of the American Red Cross.

Record Rendezvous

300 Prospect Avenue, Cleveland
142 Euclid Avenue, Cleveland

YOU CAN'T DISCUSS CLEVELAND'S rock and roll history without a close look at Leo Mintz and his store, Record Rendezvous. There's no question he was an innovator in a number of key areas. Marketing, for example. Mintz was an imposing figure, about 6 feet 4 inches, and his first shot at retail was as assistant manager in an Army-Navy surplus store. He opened his first store at 214 Prospect for just $300 in 1938, selling used jukebox records. Mintz drove to Columbus every few days to get them, and that was before freeways. Stu Mintz, his son, says that was the only way to get certain records.

"He went to the major labels, because in those days that's all there was. I remember he went to RCA, and I still have the letter they sent him at home. He needed a franchise to deal RCA records, and they wrote him back a letter: 'Dear Mr. Mintz, Thank you for your interest in RCA, but we already have a retailer in Cleveland.' Eventually he ended up buying out the guy who had the franchise. That's how it was in those days."

Leo Mintz supplied an obvious demand and did well enough to move down the street to a larger store at 300 Prospect in 1945. He was also a pioneer in self-service, putting records in racks for folks to thumb through instead of having to ask a clerk to get them from behind the counter. Later on, Mintz installed listening booths with record players so people could listen to records before buying them. Every now and then you might see one of the recording artists stop by to say hello. Then Mintz met this guy named Freed.

With all due respect to Alan Freed—and he deserves a lot—
Mintz played a critical part in those early years. He took a step
back and let a radio voice do his job, but Freed got an education on
the appeal of "race records" from the guy who sold them to a white
audience, and he sold a lot of them. In fact, music historian John
Jackson writes that when Freed had a classical music program
on WJW, he thought Mintz was crazy to want him to switch the
format of his show to rhythm and blues. But Mintz was a potential
sponsor with deep pockets and, then as now, money talks big-time.

There were reports that Mintz even sat in on some of the radio
shows and was well aware of the old term "rock and roll." It had
been used in a 1934 song on Columbia Records by the Boswell
Sisters, who sang with Jimmy Grier and His Orchestra. But Mintz
also knew the grittier definition used by black artists, and that
seemed a better fit for the stuff he was selling on WJW.

In the early 1950s, Mintz also saw the coming trend in long-play-
ing albums and the rise of home audio equipment. Problem was
LPs weren't cheap. FM radio wouldn't be commonplace for years,
so the hi-fi sound was coming off turntables. In 1955 RCA Victor
pulled the trigger on a move to drop prices on LPs from $5.98 to
$3.98. It worked. Long lines of people turned out to stock up on
records, but that $2 drop also meant a cut in profits for the stores.
Two fans of the price cuts were Mintz and WERE's Bill Randle.

Young people are pretty free with expendable cash, and rock
and roll was loosening the purse strings. Sales were up across the
board, and Mintz said, "We are getting along fabulously as a result
of the prices slashes. Turnovers in classics were tripled in the last
two months. Jazz long players did even better after bargain hunters
found they could buy five platters for the cost of three old ones."
He tipped his hat to "hi-fi addicts," and said something to a *Plain
Dealer* reporter that in retrospect seems a bit odd. Mintz believed
that if more parents encouraged their kids to have record parties
at theirs or their friends' homes, juvenile delinquency would drop
by half. Hey, street thugs like music, too!

Record Rendezvous had as many as five stores including a

Cleveland's home of rock and roll: Store owner Leo Mintz
surveys Prospect Avenue from his Record Rendezvous.
Mintz gave Alan Freed the word that kids were "rockin' and
rollin'" in the aisles of his store listening to R&B records.
(Courtesy of Janet Macoska)

smaller shop on Public Square, but the main location was 300
Prospect. That was the case even after the street had deteriorated
to a run-down running track for hookers, druggies, and other
ambassadors from the seedy underbelly of the city. Even so, there
was still plenty of pop culture along with "the 'Vous," including
Kay's Bookstore, Prospect Music, and Huron Books. At that time
there were a lot of small business people without store fronts.
Mintz still drew a lot of loyal customers. Was he aware of his role
in pop culture?

According to his son, "he was always very low-key about it. In those days many people always wanted to say, 'Leo, do something with your name. Capitalize on the fact that rock and roll began with you.' Being a very low-key person, he didn't want the notoriety. He didn't care if anyone knew it or not. When all that happened, I was very young. Maybe eight years old. As I was growing up I knew the importance of it, but not the massive importance." As he looks back at those early days, Stu says, "I wish I was 20 years older then. It's a time of my life I wish I could have seen as an adult."

It was a much simpler time, especially for a new art form. Stu says, "Rock and roll really didn't hit until the mid-'50s, when all the artists realized they had a vehicle to roll on." Did he ever talk to his dad about those days? Stu says he didn't have to. "Cleveland was the city for rock and roll. To tell the truth, over the years the topic never came up much about the importance of Cleveland because we knew matter-of-factly that Cleveland was the city. I think in those days Clevelanders were very chauvinistic about Cleveland, which we lost through the sixties. New Yorkers don't go around saying, 'We've got the most important city!' They just know it. It's a fact." Stu also tells the tale about his own Moondog-type event that had pretty much the same results.

When Stu started working the stores he had five locations around Northeast Ohio. "I got a call from Warner Brothers. This is when I had one of my stores at Richmond Mall. Freddie Katz booked the personal appearances for the label when they needed promotion for someone coming into town. He said, 'Hey! How would you like to have Leif Garrett at the store?' This was like when Leif was the teenage idol. I asked him, 'How many people do you expect?' 'Eh . . . a hundred girls.' It was like déjà vu. I had tickets to go to Disney World with my family. I said, 'Y'know . . . I'm going to be out of town, Freddie. I'm going to pass.' Ronnie Brooks was my general manager, and I left him in charge and I went to Florida. I came home a week later and saw Ronnie. He said, 'Here's what happened. Yadda yadda yadda . . . oh, and by the way, I booked Leif Garrett at Richmond Mall.' You what? Freddie

Katz had the chutzpah to call him up, figuring Ronnie would say yes even though I said no.

"Then I got a call from Sam Shapiro. He was like a godfather to me. He owned National Record Mart in Pittsburgh. The two biggest characters in the record business were Sam Shapiro and my dad, and they were very, very good friends. Sam calls me up with his low gravelly voice and he says, 'I hear you got Leif Garrett coming to your store. How many cops you got? It's not enough!' All that in one breath. Ronnie had hired two cops from Richmond Heights, and the night before, Sam had just opened up his super-store concept. It was like the Peaches stores. It was a brand-new store—and they destroyed it! So many girls showed up they broke windows, the counters, you name it. Sam tried to talk me into getting more cops quick.

"I got as many as I could. Another two. So I was sitting at my downtown office and I get a call. They closed the store at 3 in the afternoon and brought the gate halfway down because the girls were mobbing the place! The mall was overrun by hundreds and hundreds of teenage girls! They broke our showcases. Other damage, too." It was like Moondog at the mall.

Leo Mintz died in 1976. He was just 65, and he led a memorable life. The story is that he was buried with a golf club and a bottle of scotch.

In 1984, when the site search committee for the Rock and Roll Hall of Fame traveled from New York to Cleveland, the first stop on the tour was 300 Prospect Avenue.

Leo's Casino

7500 Euclid Avenue, Cleveland

THE BEST WAY TO describe the importance of Leo's Casino is as an incubator for some of the biggest musical acts. Younger readers may not know that Cleveland had a nightlife that rivaled, even exceeded, that of just about any major city of the day. On any given night in the 1950s and '60s, you could catch Cab Calloway, Jerry Van Dyke, or Jerry Vale at the Chateau Restaurant on Detroit Road; the Flamingos at the Jazz Temple on Mayfield Road; Red Buttons, Wayne Newton or Joe E. Lewis at the Theatrical on Short Vincent off East Ninth Street; or Dick Gregory and Dinah Washington and the June Taylor Dancers at the Americana Supper Club at East 16th and Euclid Avenue. Trust us. Those were huge names back then.

If there was a publicity tour, the act traveled through Northeast Ohio, and it wasn't uncommon to see folks like Jackie Gleason and bandleader Sammy Kaye stop in just to say "hi." Plus, in those days before megaplexes, all the first-run movies opened downtown. Television was still relatively new and featured a lot of local programming, there were dozens of drive-in theaters, a sirloin steak dinner cost $1.85 at Girves Brown Derby, and Cleveland had morning and afternoon newspapers.

Leo's Casino got its start at East 49th Street and Central Avenue in 1952, when it was primarily a beer joint. Owner Leo Frank had some experience booking acts for his naval base when he was in the service. He started bringing in some up-and-coming jazz acts to the bar, and Leo's started to evolve from watering hole to night spot. The club could have used a lot more water when it burned

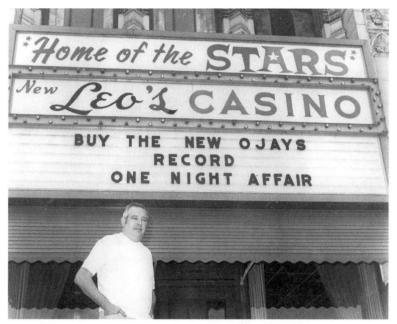

Stars shine on Euclid Avenue: Leo's Casino had a simple marquee that announced shows by some of the greatest performers of their time, in their prime. The club drew people from all parts of town, combining black and white audiences at a time when that was uncommon. *(George Shuba)*

down in 1962, but that was very likely a blessing in disguise. Frank and his partner Jules Berger opened up Leo's Casino in September 1963 at the old site of the Dobama Theatre in back of Berger's Quad Hall Lounge at East 75th and Euclid. It may have been named after one owner because using the last names of Frank and Berger would have made it sound like a hot dog place.

From the start it was billed as a nightclub, with space to seat 725 around a series of 18-inch tables. That's all the table space you needed for drinks and ashtrays. There was parking for 200 cars in a well-lit lot, and they started booking acts from day one. Now, keep in mind that this was before the media really embraced rock and roll, though that seemed almost inevitable. Leo's started packing the room with acts like Art Blakey and his Jazz Messengers, Nina

Simone, Ramsey Lewis, and Julian "Cannonball" Adderley. Joe Williams played Leo's with an act the *Plain Dealer* called "moaning the blues," saying Williams was "clean in diction and inventive in melody" and citing his time with Count Basie, Lionel Hampton, and Coleman Hawkins. Critic Glenn Fullen wasn't as kind to John Birks Gillespie, saying that with his "weird inflammatory effects" it was no wonder his nickname was "Dizzy." He called Gillespie's style weird and offbeat, and said even fans of progressive jazz couldn't explain what he was trying to say. He also suggested others were "bewildered or just irritated by his gimmicks."

Leo's became a logical stop for Motown acts. It was just a few hours from Detroit, and was the proving ground for acts on that label. Although they had a built-in fan base in the Motor City, if you couldn't impress Cleveland you needed some work. One of the first huge acts out of Detroit to play Leo's was Aretha Franklin, who was billed as one of the "greatest jazz singers" (though Columbia Records called her a "queen of the blues"). She was only 19 when she made her Cleveland debut, and even some of the hard-boiled local critics sang her praises. The *Plain Dealer* said Franklin lifted up "standard blues with the urgency and passionate appeal of a former gospel singer." That made sense. Franklin was a former gospel singer and so was her older sister Erma, whose songs were later covered by the Rolling Stones and Janis Joplin.

The club's reputation grew by the week, and when Lou Rawls set up shop in December 1963. Leo's had to run continuous shows to 5 a.m. to accommodate demand. Marvin Gaye steamrolled through a couple of weeks later as Leo's started putting more emphasis on rhythm and blues acts. Gaye had a wide audience thanks to hits like "Can I Get a Witness?" and "I'm Crazy 'Bout My Baby." Leo Frank even opened up the club for teenage matinees. Adults were welcome too, but if you were under the drinking age you were given a yellow lei to wear to tip off the waitresses.

Comedians got bookings as well, and one came with some controversy. Lincoln Perry was part of a black vaudeville team known as "Step-N-Fetchit." He was a pretty savvy guy, and the team played to urban audiences with a parody that was much like the ethnic roles in white vaudeville. Black audiences got the joke, and when the team broke up, Perry took the stage name "Stepin Fetchit." He became a major film and stage star during the Depression, and Hal Roach even filmed a pilot for a series of proposed two-reelers starring him in an Our Gang–Little Rascals film titled *A Tough Winter*. Perry made millions during the Depression and even had a limo with his name in neon lights across the back. He gave away most of his money to the needy and started to get a reputation as being difficult to work with because he demanded the same pay as his white co-stars. Sadly, white audiences didn't get the same jokes as fans in black vaudeville, and Perry's act was labeled as a racial stereotype. He updated his act to be more topical, à la Dick Gregory, and went back to nightclub work, playing Leo's Casino in early 1964.

Big changes were on the way. Top 40 radio took on a whole new personality after February 1964 when the British Invasion exploded following the Beatles' debut on the *Ed Sullivan Show*. AM stations KYW and WHK had a huge surge in listeners, but that also meant they were exposed to a lot of other acts that were already popular on urban stations like WABQ and WJMO. White audiences could now appreciate some gifted musicians who had limited play, and most of them were playing Leo's Casino. Despite the country's racial tension and civil unrest, diversity reigned at Leo's Casino as both black and white audiences enjoyed some of the rising stars in popular music. Keep in mind there was a lot of local talent as well, and acts like Akron's Ruby and the Romantics, Cleveland's Valentinos featuring Bobby Womack and his family, and the O'Jays, out of Canton, all took to Leo's Casino stage at one point in their careers.

The owners also gave back to the community when they could. Cab driver Ernest Williams had a wife and five kids aged 18 months to seven when he was killed during a robbery attempt in October 1964. The family needed winter clothing, and the future looked bleak. Frank and Berger stepped up to stage a weekend-long fund-

Talk about an intimate stage! Leo's Casino had a low ceiling, but that didn't stop performers from "raising the roof." Here, the O'Jays entertain the supper club–type crowd that was the core of Leo's clientele. *(George Shuba)*

raiser with WJMO to raise $5,000 for the family at 50 cents a head for every person coming through the club. Merchants offered goods to auction, local acts donated their talent, and a check was presented to the Williams family.

Leo's featured a lot of other promotions as well. When Solomon Burke brought his revue through town the club also featured a "Sweater Night Thursday," "Men's Night on Friday," and a Sunday "Ladies' Night." They even joined with the Continental Lounge and House of Blues (the old Gleason's) for a Big Three Picnic and a Big Three Clam Bake and steer roast to follow. They also jumped on a trend that was popping up in clubs across the country and hired two go-go girls from New York City to "shake their moneymakers" during every show at the casino.

The club also benefited from the need for local TV programming. Mike Douglas was based at KYW in Cleveland, and Herman Spero's *Big 5 Show*, which became *Upbeat* when it went to national syndication, welcomed acts visiting Cleveland; that meant free advertising for Leo's. By 1965, Leo's was riding a wave, booking top names like Mary Wells, Bobby "Blue" Bland, and standing-room-only crowds for B.B. "Blues Boy" King, topping the charts with "Rock Me Baby." Joe Tex, the Temptations, the Four Tops—you name them and they probably performed at Leo's, a hot spot well into 1966. The acts played to a sophisticated supper club-type audience, and at least one performer found out the hard way that you didn't step over that line.

That July, the Supremes were booked for a six-day engage-ment of three shows a night, creating a rare opportunity to see a top-rated act that played much bigger rooms across the country. Tickets went fast thanks to the group's success on TV, radio, and stage appearances. This was also a double bill with a young comic named Flip Wilson as opening act and emcee. Even Motown Records head Berry Gordy came to Cleveland for the show, but he didn't like what came out of Wilson's mouth. Word is that Wilson had some pretty edgy material and Gordy stormed backstage to let him know in some very strong language that kind of entertainment didn't fly. You also knew not to cross Berry Gordy.

That Supremes show was also special for a local kid named Gene Shelton, who would later rise to top media and publicity jobs at Motown and Warner Brothers Records. He tells us he'd seen the Supremes once before, not on a stage. "The first time I ever saw the Supremes was not at Leo's. They were at a Giant Tiger store on Euclid Avenue. I took every Supremes album I had and stood in line to get their autographs." Shelton was a teenager and really wanted to see this show, but he wasn't sure he could get through the door. "This was the first time the Supremes appeared at Leo's. Being a minor I didn't think they would let me in because they served alcohol, so I asked my mother to take me. That opening night I walked into Leo's with my mother, and they either gave me a wrist band or a lei to say, 'You're welcome to stay, but you can't serve this child alcohol.' I remember when the Supremes came on opening night. Usually the artist opened at Leo's on a Thursday, did Friday and Saturday, and then a matinee and evening show on Sunday. The policy was usually open on a Friday and close after two shows on Sunday. The Supremes were such a huge act that they had a six-night stand. And the show! Being so close and seeing them interact with the audience." For Shelton, Leo's Casino was the Copa! He also remembers a lot of local history occurring just a few blocks away.

"The Glenville race riots were happening when the Supremes were at Leo's. The club stayed open, and I remember Flip Wilson was their opening act. I thought, 'What was happening here?' I'm looking at these three women who I love, and I asked the manager if I could come back tomorrow. He said, 'Sure, as long as you wear that band. You don't need mommy!' I had a little job working at a hospital, and I used everything in my bank account to see the Supremes. I don't believe the Supremes stayed the full time they were booked because the riots kept escalating. Maybe it was Leo, or even Berry Gordy, but someone thought the city was too dangerous, especially after what happened up in Detroit with the riots there." Whatever the reason, it was a night that would change Gene Shelton's life, and when he got to Motown he got to write about it when he crafted the liner notes for the album *The Supremes Greatest Hits*.

Leo's Casino was pulling in some serious money, but the owners knew they had to stay a step ahead to stay on top. They closed down for a few weeks and did a major remodeling job on the Quad Hall Lounge and Casino that included a new bandstand for the lounge, aimed at a new policy of 52 shows a year. To cover the cost when the ribbon was cut in October 1966, the owners established a 50-cent cover charge for the shows in the lounge. There was a contest, too, with a $50 top prize to rename the lounge, but some thought the act chosen to re-open the casino was a bit odd. The owners booked Wayne Cochran and the C.C. Riders, a group of white "blue-eyed soul brothers" headed by a shouter with a high,

Leo's Casino was a natural meeting place for notables visiting the city. (From L to R): Leo Frank, activist Ruth Turner, comedian Dick Gregory, and house emcee Freddie Arrington in 1969. *(Cleveland Public Library)*

bleached-blond bouffant hairdo. Cochran was a favorite at clubs around the country, and it was anyone's guess how the Leo's crowd would take to him.

The owners appealed to a wide audience but aimed for an upper-tier patron with expendable cash. Enter Freddie Arrington Sr., an enterprising car salesman at Thompson's House of Fine Cars on Kinsman Road, who promised customers a night on the town at Leo's for giving him their business. The Thompson folks had worked with Leo's Casino transporting folks in their Jaguar Celebrity Car for "red carpet treatment" with "many special delicacies." You could see the Jag in front of Leo's for most of the engagements.

The big names kept appearing on the marquee. Etta James, Jimmy Ruffin, Dionne Warwick, and more were added through the 1966 season, though one act was deemed a bit steamy for the usual teen matinee: the Ike and Tina Turner Revue. In their early performances, the audience sweated as much as the band, a group with heavy sexual overtones that packed the room every show.

The teen matinees continued into 1967 with Smokey Robinson and the Miracles and other acts, and Frank and Berger kept a close eye to make sure no alcohol would get into underage hands. One popular act kept booze out of adult hands, too. Anyone who runs a club can tell you that liquor is a huge money maker, but when the Staple Singers came through with their "gospel cavalcade," the club was dry for the four-night run. Some acts were too young to drink, like "Little Stevie" Wonder, who had just turned 17 when he was booked at Leo's. He even had to apply for a work permit from the city before he could take the stage.

That year came to end with a historic and tragic December performance that stunned the music world.

Otis Redding was thrilling audiences across the globe. He had huge hits on the R&B charts as a solo artist and with "Tramp," his duet with Carla Thomas, but onstage, this guy was on fire. Take a look at his explosive performance in the 1968 movie *Monterey Pop*, filmed at the festival of the same name, and he tore it up on a "Memphis Sound" European tour with other Stax Records artists. Redding was on the edge of superstardom and his tour schedule was relentless. Just days after laying down the tracks for a new single everyone thought would be his pop breakthrough, Redding and his backup band, the Bar Kays, flew into Cleveland in his Beechcraft H18 tour plane. He raced over to the WEWS studios for a taping of the *Upbeat* show and apologized to the producers for being late due to problems with his plane. He performed a couple of songs at the taping, including a version of Eddie Floyd's "Knock on Wood" with Detroit's Mitch Ryder. After doing one Leo's Casino show that night of December 9, he and the band boarded the plane in bad weather heading to Wisconsin, crashing into Lake Monona near Madison just a short time later. Wreckage of the plane is on display at the Rock and Roll Hall of Fame. Sure enough, the song he recorded was released just a few weeks later and did become his breakthrough hit. "(Sittin' on) The Dock of the Bay" was a departure from his usual soul style, and those in the audience at Leo's were among the first and last to hear it live.

The show must go on, and it did at Leo's Casino during the Christmas '67 season with the start of special Wednesday "Freak Out Nites" with psychedelic lights and go-go girls. The top names kept coming through, and comedians were turning out to be a draw. They included "Moms" Mabley, ventriloquist Willie Tyler and Lester, and the Cleveland debut of Richard "Dick" Pryor, sharing a bill with Martha Reeves and the Vandellas.

The economics were changing, however, as top names with hit songs began to command higher prices and perform in larger venues, including arenas. Sam and Dave, Gladys Knight and the Pips, and other names were still being booked, but Leo's also had to schedule fashion shows and charity shows to get people in seats. By the spring of 1969 the number of available acts dwindled and the lights went out at Leo's Casino. The front lounge stayed open for a time with food and drink, and there were efforts to reopen the casino, but you need name acts to draw, and such acts had moved on to bigger things. In 1983, Leo Frank had talks with restaurateur Jim Swingos about opening a version of the club at the Statler Office Tower, but without the people who made it happen on stage, you couldn't recapture the magic.

Still, the memories of Leo's Casino endure.

In September 1995, former Supreme Mary Wilson was in town for the opening of the Rock and Roll Hall of Fame and Museum. She asked her driver to take a side trip to East 75th and Euclid Avenue. The Leo's Casino building was long gone, and Wilson got out of the car and looked at the empty lot. There were quiet moments, a smile, and she got back in the car. A few years later the Rock Hall declared the site a Cleveland landmark and erected a plaque summarizing its place in history. It's now the location of a supermarket, a far cry from the nightclub that launched the superstars of R&B.

La Cave

LEGENDS GROW WITH TIME, and the stories that surround La Cave are a prime example. No, Bob Dylan never played there, and don't believe anyone who swears he did. Neither did Joan Baez or Peter, Paul and Mary, though Mary Travers might have stopped in, and maybe, just maybe, Eric Clapton did, too. We'll get to that in a bit, but let's start at a time when a lot of amazing musicians made big noise with acoustic guitars.

The story begins in January 1962 in an old basement pool hall under the Social Security office at the northeast corner of East 105th Street and Euclid Avenue. The area used to be called the Doan's Corner Theater District, with plenty of movie houses, restaurants, and night clubs in what many considered Cleveland's second downtown. During the golden age of vaudeville, top names would perform at Playhouse Square, and a week later they would set up shop a few miles east at University Circle. The Alhambra, the Circle, and Keith's 105th were all there. Come the mid-1960s and there were mostly bars, with hookers leaving doorways to run out to the street to advertise their "goods." Even though the district had seen better days, three partners had an upbeat idea.

Stan Heilbrun, Nelson Karl, and Lee Weiss saw a coming trend. Heilbrun came out of the Cleveland Institute of Music and had an impressive collection of musical instruments. He also gave private guitar lessons. Karl was a student of his; Weiss was another guitar student brought in as an investor.

It came up in conversation that it would cost about $912 to open a coffeehouse at University Circle. Popular music was in transition. The first era of rock and roll had started to fade with some of the biggest names—Buddy Holly, Richie Valens, and the Big Bopper, J.R. Richardson—dying in a plane crash. Chuck Berry was in prison, Little Richard joined the clergy, Jerry Lee Lewis saw his career go up in smoke when the press found out he had married a 13-year-old cousin, and Elvis Presley was inducted into the Army. When Presley got out he was a different kind of entertainer, and it took years for him to be a rock and roll singer again. At the same time, something new was happening in tiny clubs and college campuses.

Folk music had been around a long time, but when the 1960s hit, its profile began to rise. The post-World War II Beat Generation blossomed. Writers like William S. Burroughs, Allen Ginsberg, and Jack Kerouac spawned a new, beatnik counterculture. The Beat writers offered insight, but musicians gave them voice. Pete Seeger, Woody Guthrie, the Weavers, and dozens of other acts put to music the dissent over civil rights, the Viet Nam War, and McCarthy-era politics. College campuses were a breeding ground for protest, and students looked for places to make their opinions heard. In 1961, that place was born near East 105th and Euclid and was called La Cave, or to be technical, La Cave de Café, Inc.

Three more people tell the La Cave story best: Stan Kain, Larry Bruner, and Steve Traina.

Bruner describes La Cave as: "a basement concert coffeehouse with rickety tables and some mismatched chairs. Attentive, listening audiences who sat through the shows were the norm. It was not what one would term a 'rock and roll venue,' because no one ever got up and danced. A Day-Glo mural telling people to 'Feed Your Head' filled one wall. We served espresso, baklava, later on 3.2 beer and potato chips. As 'Cleveland's House of Folk Music,' we generally featured acoustic solo acts, with the occasional blues band, and even more occasionally, the odd blues/rock group."

As Kain recalls, "It opened in 1961 as a coffee shop with poetry. They weren't making it, and I knew the three people who started it and came to them with the idea to make it into a folk music place." It made sense because Kain was more than just an idea man. He

At the center of Cleveland's folk scene, La Cave catered to a college crowd from nearby universities as well as music lovers from across Northeast Ohio. Major names such as Gordon Lightfoot got their first U.S. exposure at the club. *(Stan Kain collection)*

brought a résumé saying, "I actually got my start in my early 20s working at Cain Park Theatre in the early days before that. By 1962 they were getting ready to close because they weren't making enough to even pay the rent. I told them I had an idea, and they said, 'If you can make a go of it we'll make you a partner.'" Kain's idea went way beyond poetry.

"I went in with my father and rebuilt the place—stage, lighting, sound. We started booking just local people for a few weeks. We called them 'hootenannies.' I went to a fellow I knew that managed

Bob Gibson, whom I met at Faragher's Back Room up in Cleveland Heights. I told him I was thinking about booking folk acts, and he put me in touch with his manager, and that guy asked me about booking Josh White. I liked Josh White, and I agreed to pay him $450 for shows on Friday, Saturday, and Sunday. The partners all said, '$450!? That's going to break us completely! We'll be out of business!'"

Traina says, "Keep in mind that was a lot more than a month's rent back then. In today's dollars it's the equivalent of $3,600." That's a lot of money to generate in a coffee house that seated around 300. Simple math would tell you that you had to sell a whole lot of coffee, and this was no Starbucks.

Kain was sure it would work.

"I told them we could do very well, and I went to the newspapers and radio stations. Opening day we had lines down the street and around the corner. They told me, 'You take over. We're not going to have anything to do with it, and we're going to make you an equal partner.' They dropped one of the other partners and said, 'You can manage it. You can run it!' They were so blown out of the water by that first weekend. We started with Josh White and used local people from the hootenannies for the opening acts."

The partner who left was Stan Heilbrun, who left to start his own business, a head shop.

The question was, how do you keep the folkies coming back for more?

Word got around pretty quickly that La Cave was the place, but that also meant putting quality people on stage to keep people coming through the door. Was there a circuit? Kain says, "After we started booking acts I would go to New York about every three months and stay in Greenwich Village. I hit all the clubs like the Village Gate, Gerde's Folk City. I'd check them out and talk to the acts about coming to Cleveland." The artists were happy to have a place to play in what was still a major city. Plus, there was plenty of local up-and-coming talent. Kain recalls, "Brewer & Shipley were high school age when they first played La Cave," but Traina is quick to add, "Mike Brewer had played there solo. He's from Kansas City, and Shipley is from Bedford. They actually met in Kent at the Blind Owl. They ended up playing at La Cave. When they played the La Cave reunion in 2010 they told the story about being on Nixon's enemies list." In those days that was a badge of honor. Kain points out that, "La Cave was on Nixon's list! It was because of the people we had, people like Phil Ochs, the protest singer. They were considered enemies of America." Let's say some of the acts of that day were unique in peculiar ways. Buffy Saint-Marie was an American Indian who played a mouth bow and sang protest songs based on the Native American experience. Jesse Fuller was known to travel the country in a rattletrap car and played a bass fiddle with foot pedals he called a "futdilla." There also was a thriving folk scene across the border in Canada.

As Kain tells it, "We were having an act named Ian and Sylvia from Canada, and they called and said they had their own opening act. I told them, 'If you think he's good enough to open for you, that would be fine.' It turned out to be Gordon Lightfoot, and it was the first time he played in the United States."

Traina adds, "He announced on stage it was his first U.S. club engagement. Stan has a recording of it."

Wait a minute. A recording?

"Yeah, I taped most of the shows. My other business was a little studio that did TV commercials and industrial films, so I had good recording equipment. It blows my mind when I listen to them now." The recordings are near-studio quality, and Stan Kain had the foresight to keep them all these years. "I just loved the folk scene. It was just a part-time job, and La Cave was just an evening gig. We had a lot of big names. Odetta came out to my house and swam in my pool on a Sunday. Josh White came out for a picnic." There was an obvious camaraderie, a family built on common ground and trust. Almost every act that played La Cave was recorded by Kain with the artist's knowledge and approval. But he also shut down the machines when asked.

Gordon Lightfoot was working on his first big hit, "Early

Morning Rain," when he played La Cave. He even worked on it at
a Cleveland Heights apartment Kain kept for the artists. Quoting
Kain, Traina says, "He told me the story that was backed up by the
recordings that when Lightfoot was playing that night he said,
'OK, Stan. I need you to turn the tape recorder off.' Unfortunately,
Stan complied." But that also was evidence of the trust that kept
people coming back to play La Cave. It was a great opportunity to
see amazing acts in their formative years like Simon and Garfunkel, Jose Feliciano, Tim Buckley, and Phil Ochs, all happy to set
up shop at La Cave. Even so, there was the occasional difficult act.

"Flatt and Scruggs," Kain says, "had to have everything separate.
They had to have two different dressing rooms, and they came in
separately, too. The only time they got together was on the stage.
They were enemies!" So you had folk, and in Flatt and Scruggs's
case, bluegrass. La Cave offered a lot of different kinds of music,
and diversity, both musical and racial, was a key to its success. Sax-
ophonist Albert Ayler was such a unique experimental jazz artist,
some thought he had never picked up an instrument, even though
he started the same song the same way every time he played it.

Traina says, "It was on the edge of the Case university campus
before Case merged with Western Reserve University. You had a
lot of people from the Case campus, and the club had always been
integrated. In that respect, Stan was colorblind to race in that club
on stage or in the audience."

During this period, race relations in most urban areas were
strained, to say the least. Even so, Kain says that in the early days,
"When it started to get busy we would do a couple of shows a
night. We'd make everyone leave after the first show and set up for
the second. People used to sit around all night. Good mixture of
people, too, from the suburbs and the city. The only time anyone
was afraid was when they had the riots. We had police out front for
that. At the end of 1962 when the Cuban Missile Crisis was happening, my brother put a sign up that said, 'The only bombshells
here are entertainers on our stage!'" You got to see a lot of major
acts who were just starting out, too.

Many of them stayed at a place Kain kept just for visiting artists. "I had an apartment on Hampshire Road in Cleveland Heights. Linda Ronstadt with the Stone Poneys stayed there, and Cass Elliott stayed there when she was with two other groups than the Mamas and the Papas—The Big Three and the Triumvirate. They felt comfortable there."

People would show up out of nowhere. "Bill Randle showed up at my house one night and I didn't know who he was. We were having a party with Tom Paxton, and there was a knock on the door. 'Hi, my name is Bill Randle and I hear you're having all these people play tonight.' Buzzy Linhart and Bob Gibson were there, too. Stuff like that happened all the time." The acts kept coming to Cleveland, too.

"It's different how you book acts today," Traina says. "Back then most of the acts would book Tuesday through Sunday, six days. But Gordon Lightfoot would play here for a week and get held over for another week, so they might make $300 or $400, but it would be for a dozen shows." He knows what he's talking about, too, because Kain kept all the contracts from his time at the club and Traina has access to all of them.

There was also a good deal of politics to running a club, and you had to work the system. Kain recalls, "About halfway through the '60s we got a 3.2 beer license. We tried for a year to get that beer license and they wouldn't give it to us. Finally, someone came down and told us, 'If you give him a hundred dollars he can make sure you get that license,' and a week later we had it! It wasn't a bar. All we served was 3.2 beer. We never wanted to do anything further than that. We had a little kitchen where we served sandwiches. I bought most of my stuff from Irv's Delicatessen in Cleveland Heights on Coventry. He gave me a good price, and that was how we made our food service."

As Bob Dylan sang "The Times They Are A-Changin'," local folk historian Dick Minke wrote that the Cleveland folk scene was starting to fade by 1966. Kain was willing to stage any act he thought would appeal to the audience, and there was a load of rising talent from both the U.S. and abroad. He decided to give some early rock acts a try. "I heard them, enjoyed them, and thought I would try them. It sure didn't hurt our income. Blues Project had evolved into Blood, Sweat & Tears, and one day I got a call from their manager, and he said, 'We'll come and work for a weekend free if you let us have a press publicity party on Thursday.' Great! Thursday was all theirs, and the weekend was all for us. Al Kooper was with them at that time, not David Clayton-Thomas."

Big names, too. "Jeff Beck and Rod Stewart played there with the Jeff Beck Group. They stayed at my apartment and slept on my floor. One of them rolled me a joint the size of a cigar, and I think I smoked it for a year." And there were acts La Cave made stars. "Hello People were huge. People would send me letters asking to see them back at the club as soon as they were available." Their promotion man Lew Futterman was one of them.

Larry Bruner had been a regular patron of La Cave over the years and knew some of the record promotion people and even the acts that played the Versailles Motor Inn on Euclid. Bruner worked the desk there overnights to put himself through college, and some top names would play the hotel's supper club and penthouse. Many of the acts ended up on the syndicated *Upbeat* show on WEWS just down the street, so there was a lot happening at the Versailles. When Bruner graduated from John Carroll University in August 1967 he started looking for a gig in entertainment law. Nelson Karl and Stan Kain interviewed and hired him over lunch, and Karl reportedly said, "I don't understand why someone like him would want to come work for us."

That was at the tail end of the "Summer of Love," and hippies didn't have a lot of money. Even so, to keep the club open the staff tightened up the list at the door, making everyone pony up the $3 cover charge. No more tabs for pitchers of beer either.

Bruner started designing monthly postcards with psychedelic lettering that went out to patrons on the mailing list. There was other overhead as well. Cleveland was a union town, and reps from the American Federation of Musicians dropped by every week to

Move over folkies! The club near East 105th Street and Euclid Avenue later mixed in rock acts like Neil Young and Crazy Horse, Jeff Beck, and many more playing to a small room packed with people sipping pitchers of draft beer.

look over contracts and make sure the club contributed to the local's health and welfare fund.

In 1967, Kain also lined up an unknown guitarist from England through a block booking arrangement with a guy described as "a dubious Columbus agent." It was Jimi Hendrix, six weeks before his American debut at the Monterey International Pop Festival. The LP "Are You Experienced?" had been released, and Bruner, who was in the audience, let out an audible gasp when Kain announced the booking. Bruner had seen an advance screening of the Monterey film and was eagerly awaiting the show, but it was not to be—at least, not at La Cave. Hendrix instead performed some months later, in March 1968 at Cleveland Music Hall.

One of the enduring La Cave legends involves an alleged 1968 visit by Eric Clapton, then touring with Cream. Records show the band left New York on May 9 for shows at the Akron Civic Theater and Cleveland Music Hall on May 11 and 12. The band had a free day in Cleveland on the 10th and there were stories that Clapton stopped at La Cave to sit in with the group Mandala featuring Domenic Troiano, a Canadian guitarist who would later play in the James Gang. There are, however, no photos or newspaper reports, and Steve Traina continues to chase down possible leads.

So how did La Cave get some of those top rock names? Well, weekends were gold for club owners, and bigger cities were able to book major names, knowing they were cash cows. Clubs like La Cave were able to book midweek at lower fees when the acts were on the road between dates at the huge clubs. Besides Jeff Beck, other big names that played La Cave included Arthur Lee's Love, Ten Years After, the Butterfield Blues Band, Ultimate Spinach, the Blues Magoos, the Fugs, Canned Heat, Terry Knight and the Pack, Moby Grape, the Nazz (with Todd Rundgren), and Procol Harum. Iron Butterfly played its first gig away from the West Coast at La Cave, and Atco Records' national promotions director thanked Bruner for bringing the band to his attention—though it already had two albums out. Its second LP included "In-A-Gadda-Da-Vida," a huge hit after it was edited down to single length.

Blood, Sweat & Tears spent the entire week at La Cave rehearsing for what would become their second album. The Velvet Underground called La Cave one of the few places outside New York City that understood what they were all about, and a bootleg recording of the band's La Cave gig floated around for years. A segment even showed up on an official VU retrospective. There were some that were a lot more difficult to book.

Joni Mitchell was getting a lot of attention in 1968, and La Cave booked her three times. The club even advertised her once, but each time she was a no-show. Bruner went to the Miami International Pop Festival later that year and caught up with Albert Grossman to talk about The Hawks, who would later be known as The Band. Mitchell happened to be there, and as luck would have it, Bruner brought along one of her signed contracts, which he showed her when he introduced himself. Mitchell was with a man named Elliot Roberts—like Grossman, a famous manager of rock groups—and she asked him, "Do you know anything about this?" Despite the tension and the fact that Roberts didn't answer why the gigs were canceled, Roberts did establish a relationship with Bruner that brought Neil Young to La Cave twice in the next six months. Kain speculates that Mitchell might have canceled because she didn't like to fly. Other high-profile cancellations included Traffic, Big Brother and the Holding Company, and Soft Machine.

Some very strange things started to happen around La Cave and the community it served in the spring of 1968. On Monday, May 13, Bruner arrived at the club to find the front door broken and an FBI search warrant on the steps. The headlines the next day told the story. The feds claimed to have broken wide open the University Circle supply line for LSD, downers, speed, and marijuana, based on a similar bust in Kent. Agents went undercover as pushers and said they had handled more than a million dollars' worth of acid before they swooped in for the arrests. Four people were arrested, including Kain. Bob Rotatori, the assistant U.S. attorney, said agents targeted the suppliers rather than the users, collecting an estimated $20,000 in LSD and other drugs during the raids. The others arrested included a podiatrist, a soft drink salesman, and an insurance agent, all charged with violating the Drug Abuse Control Act of 1966. That was the law passed after Congressional hearings on the potential dangers of LSD.

Bad news moves newspapers, and the press was all over this. Kain denied that LSD was ever distributed in his club, though he would not deny that some folks took diet pills, which were amphetamines. The podiatrist admitted he did prescribe amphetamines, but only for his wife and himself, and Rotatori suggested the alleged drug sales were strictly for profit and not personal use. Those were the days when "black beauties" and other forms of speed were commonly prescribed.

The charges claimed that drugs would be left and later picked up in a locker at the Severance Shopping Center in Cleveland Heights. Some parts of the charges seem odd. For example, the drugs were reportedly sold on consignment. What dealer sells on consignment? They were trusted to bring back cash and divvy it up. The agents also said they had handled as much as three-and-a-half ounces of LSD, or about 350,000 trips. They sold for anywhere from $2 to $10 a hit on the open market. The LSD was said to have been imported from the West Indies, with more expected to come in from London. Why would those charged look for that type of drug from overseas when just about any chemistry student could cook up a batch in their kitchen? Also, Augustus Owsley Stanley on the West Coast was said to have generated at least a million doses and had a network to move a whole lot of illegal drugs. Nothing against the feds; they don't make a move unless they can back it up, but there were obvious questions.

Did Kain decide to leave La Cave? "I didn't decide. The police decided for me. I got two-to-fifteen for the drug charge. A couple of months later it became a misdemeanor and they let me go. They were always coming down to the club saying, 'We know this act is smoking marijuana and might have drugs. Please call us.' How many acts are going to come to your club if you call the police on them? I minded my business, though I did smoke with them, and we kept hard drugs away. Police said, 'If you don't help us we're going to get you!' It was the very end of 1968, and they got me."

Bruner was now in charge, and the staff used the headlines to generate their own publicity. Acid was a part of daily life for the hippie community. Granted, a dangerous one, but that didn't stop people from getting what they wanted. A group called the Apple Pie Motherhood Band asked from the stage, "Who wants some LSD?," and the staff even used the story to advertise an upcoming show by Dr. John, "The Night Tripper." They wrapped a few thousand sugar cubes with a paper that plugged the show and a "p.s." that claimed every tenth cube was dosed with LSD. Of course they weren't, but La Cave people handed them out on street corners and what people did after that they did at their own risk.

Now, about Dr. John. Bruner recalls, "Dr. John was a very disappointing draw for his first of two nights, did a sloppy performance, and was asking staff for heroin. He was the only act I ever told to leave. He was paid for one night only."

Another emerging act that played La Cave was the New York Rock and Roll Ensemble. The five-piece band included three former Julliard students, among them Michael Kamen. He would go on to work with members of Pink Floyd, Eric Clapton, Queen, David Bowie, and many others.

Oh yes, Johnny Winter. La Cave booked Winter for three nights in the late spring of 1969 with a $3,500 guarantee. As Bruner tells it, they would be the last shows scheduled at La Cave before it closed. Winter was starting to get a lot of attention, and out of nowhere he canceled the gig. He was later advertised for a show at Cleveland Music Hall. Bruner says, "Nelson [Karl] was outraged and sued for the contract price, won a judgment, and went down with the sheriff and got the Music Hall gate receipts confiscated. We collected!"

So why did La Cave shut its doors?

With the birth of FM free-form progressive rock radio, the market for many of these acts seemed wide open. WNCR, WMMS, and many college stations played folk, hard rock, and just about anything in between, the same acts that were breaking at La Cave. But the live music was shifting from Public Square down the midtown corridor to the second downtown at University Circle.

Bruner says, "After the Glenville disturbance [in late July 1968], our core white audience from the Heights suburbs seemed to dry up. Leo's Casino, at 7500 Euclid Avenue, was our canary in the coal mine to signal that. They stopped booking traveling acts in January 1969. We held on 'til July." People were afraid to come into the city at certain hours. And then the curtain was drawn. La Cave was no more.

Let's consider the legacy.

Over the years, La Cave had booked Jeff Beck, Butterfield Blues Band, Arlo Guthrie, Richie Havens, Tim Hardin, Ten Years After, Blood, Sweat & Tears, Iron Butterfly, Canned Heat, Neil Young, Hugh Romney ("Wavy Gravy"), and Sweetwater. All were signed to play Woodstock just two months after La Cave closed, though Beck didn't show at Yasgur's farm. Jimi Hendrix, Johnny Winter, Big Brother and the Holding Company, and Joni Mitchell never made their La Cave dates, though with the exception of Mitchell, who became stuck in traffic, all were also booked into and played at Woodstock.

Larry Bruner is quick to talk at length about the "drama, rebellion, humor" that defined rock and folk. Stan Kain and Steve Traina still get out to shows, mostly acts that played La Cave many years ago. Traina will pick up Kain, who always doubts anyone will remember him. They'll enjoy the show, and afterward they will stand in line to say hello to the artist. They're not in line long, because the act they came to see will drop everything to greet them and relive the old days. Judy Collins has called out to Kain from the stage, and Arlo Guthrie stopped an autograph session to share a few memories backstage. They're part of a legacy Cleveland sometimes fought to destroy, but now embraces as part of its rich musical heritage.

The Coliseum at Richfield

2923 Streetsboro Road, Richfield Township

YEAH, WE KNOW THE Coliseum was about halfway between Cleveland and Akron and way outside the city limits of either. Still, it was the only hall around big enough to attract the biggest touring acts, and that's just what it did. Can we cover all the shows that played there? Not even in a book twice this size. But certain concerts helped elevate the Coliseum to near-mythical status. Let's take a look.

First, a little history. Nick Mileti was a well-heeled businessman who had a big piece of the Cleveland Cavaliers (and, later, the Cleveland Indians). The city was happy to have a basketball team when the Cavaliers arrived in 1970. But the Cleveland Arena, where they played, was a downer. The Arena was like Gene Carroll on WEWS-TV. You loved them, there was a lot of history, but you never pictured either one them ever being young. Visiting teams likened the Arena to the Black Hole of Calcutta. Maybe it was time to move.

Mileti decided that Richfield Township looked like the place. And was going to put out some serious cash. Original estimates showed a new arena would cost $17 million, which swelled to $25 million before the doors opened.

Fans, however, were griping about the location before the first shovel turned dirt. Richfield? Where is that? Why there? A Cleveland firm called Business Research Services found in 1973 that nearly 62 percent of people surveyed wanted the new arena building downtown, for convenience. Some said such a venue could be key to reviving downtown Cleveland and could serve more people.

But some saw the city as unsafe and said Richfield might be a good idea. A lot of folks who responded to that survey had visited the Arena in recent months and based their response on experience.

Lots of people had opinions, but Mileti had the money and the teams, so Richfield it was. Work began, and the opening date was set for October 26, 1974. When you have an idea that's larger than life, you need something bigger than a truck pull for a grand opening. The first act to play the Coliseum was Frank Sinatra, and it was like a Hollywood premiere. Green and blue lights criss-crossed the building, and champagne flowed everywhere, but the payoff came after the concert. Mileti held a post-show party for 2,000 and the corks kept popping into the night. William Eels was there. He was chairman of the board of governors for Blossom Music Center, which was right down the road. He congratulated Mileti on his successful opening, joking, "Of course, I'd like to burn the place down, but I'll resist." The Coliseum would be big-time competition for Blossom in the summer months.

Bugs still had to be worked out. Traffic congestion was something else, and when cars came to a standstill on the freeways, there were always people riding the berms seeking to cut in. Still, major acts now had options in Northeast Ohio. Who would be the first to rock the Coliseum stage?

Well before the opening there was speculation whether Stevie Wonder would bring his tour to Cleveland. He was at a career high and had opened for the Rolling Stones at the Akron Rubber Bowl in 1972. Wonder was enjoying critical acclaim, and there was a rumor he would appear at Public Hall in September '74. Not so. On October 28 he became the first rock artist to headline the Coliseum, with Chaka Khan and Rufus as opening act. Wonder told the crowd, "I've been away too long," and 10,000 people agreed. There were a few glitches. Huge screens showed close-ups of the stage, but the sound mix was less than stellar. Some complained that for the high ticket prices they paid—$9 a head—they should be able to hear the show. One fan from Dallas asked the *PD*'s Jane Scott, "How can you possibly have good acoustics with the ceiling as high

The Big House on the Prairie: The Coliseum was built seemingly in the middle of nowhere between Akron and Cleveland to attract crowds from across Northeast Ohio. Drawing crowds wasn't a problem. Traffic often was. *(Cleveland Press Collection, Cleveland State University Archives)*

as this?" People in the loges said the music was directed to lower levels, so audio engineers had their work cut out for them. There were other shows scheduled, but the big one was just a couple of months away.

The Beatles had broken up five years earlier, but they were all very productive with their individual careers and still drew major attention for anything they did. George Harrison was the first former Beatle to announce a solo tour, and the Richfield Coliseum date was December 2nd. It sold out almost immediately, and another show was added for the same night at 10:15. Same thing, tickets gone. However, the promoters faced an unanticipated roadblock: Mother Nature. Midwest winters started early in those days, and Harrison's tour got snowed in at Chicago. Northeast Ohio never got to see the tour, but by most accounts the fans didn't miss much. Harrison's voice was strained, and reviews from other stops were tepid at best.

Things started to get a little weird a few months after the ribbon was cut. In February 1975, Governor James Rhodes had a notion to make Ohio "depression proof," and part of that involved $2.5 billion in construction projects for the Greater Cleveland area. That would keep tradesmen busy for a couple of years, but what would they build? How about a $40 million "mini-domed" arena seating 20,000 next to Municipal Stadium? People looked at this plan and rubbed their eyes. Another Coliseum? Come on. Even Dorothy Fuldheim over at WEWS thought that was a ridiculous idea. She asked, "If another coliseum is built, what happens to Nick Mileti's Coliseum in Richfield? There is just so much in entertainment activities that any community can support, you know." Big Red, as she was known, was right, and the Ohio Legislature brought that idea to an end.

The big shows would keep coming in Summit County, and plenty did. We warned you we can't cover all of them, a long list including Electric Light Orchestra, the Eagles, the Who with Keith Moon on drums. Let's focus on a few.

By the time he came to the Coliseum, Elvis Presley was a glorified lounge act, but his fans didn't care. He was still "the King," or, as comic Steve Harvey, a Cleveland native, would say, "the Kang." Glittery jumpsuits, a couple of chins, and a big potbelly were the look, but underneath it all he was still "Elvis the Pelvis." He knew how to put on the big show, and he came to Richfield to do just that. It was summer 1975 and there was such demand for tickets after an immediate sellout left long lines, the Coliseum booked a second show.

The first was set for July 10, the other eight days later. Mileti made it a point to be at the show because this was Elvis Presley and he wanted to make sure everything was perfect before he went on stage. Mileti was happy to report that both manager Colonel Tom Parker and Presley were easy to work with. No major demands in the contract rider, but he did ask a favor—the dressing room nearest the stage. Anything you need, pal.

The day of the show was more like a circus than a concert. There were souvenir tables lining the hallways with programs, posters, records, and just about anything that could accommodate Presley's name. But let's face it. You were there for the show!

Presley was 40 years old, and folks wondered if age had caught up with him. The night of the show his backup band warmed up the crowd, the dramatic "Also Sprach Zarathustra" theme from *2001: A Space Odyssey* played, and then . . . there he was! A big guy in a cape and sequined jumpsuit, with hair way too black to be natural. He walked backward a lot, and started the show with "C.C. Rider." He held the crowd in his hands. Those were the days of little Instamatic cameras with 110-film cartridges and flash cubes. People in the back rows were snapping one photo after another and the Coliseum pulsated with light from those tiny cameras for the entire show. Presley didn't look like the old "hillbilly cat," but that voice seemed to get better over the years. He told corny jokes you were obliged to laugh at, did a bunch of karate moves, kissed lots of girls, and threw out lots of cheap, sweaty scarves. It was everything you hoped for!

He wore the guitar more than he played it, but people came to hear him sing and Presley knocked out 21 songs in an hour. He knew which side his bread was buttered on, too. You want the hits? How about "All Shook Up," "Teddy Bear," "Love Me Tender," "Burning Love," and even a couple of covers of songs by Olivia Newton-John? Who cared what he sang? This was the guy they called "the King" before LeBron James, and James probably couldn't pull off sequins and a cape.

There was "How Great Thou Art" and "Why Me, Lord" for the gospel fans, and "The Wonder of You" that Presley joked he recorded "25 or 30 years ago." Bruno Bornino of the *Cleveland Press* noted that when Presley asked for the house lights to go up so he could read the signs, he pointed one out that said, "One kiss or I'll die." Well, he couldn't have that. He did that Presley sneer and called out, "I can't let you die, come on down and get your kiss." Gangway! Plus, she got a red rose to remember the moment (as if she would forget).

A few more songs, and Presley started sifting through the stuff

Start spreadin' the news: "Ol' Blue Eyes" himself, Frank
Sinatra, opened the Coliseum for its first show. Concertgoers
also got a souvenir medallion to mark the occasion.

that got thrown on stage for his approval, and—what's this?! Black
bikini panties, which he wrapped around the head of one of his
band members. Presley ended the show with the song "King of
the Mountain." The music swelled, Presley and a bunch of people
started waving goodbye, and a few minutes after he left the stage
the lights came up and the PA announcer stated, "Ladies and gentlemen, Elvis has left the building." That was your cue to do the
same. Those two shows wouldn't be the last time Elvis played the
Coliseum. That happened on October 23, 1976. Ten months later,
he left us forever.

Another show, in 1976, got a huge response. Paul McCartney and Wings had released the classic LP *Band on the Run*, followed by *Venus and Mars*. It was time to take the show on the road, and a May 10 gig was arranged for the Coliseum.

The fourth date on the tour was something of a homecoming for Linda McCartney. Her mother, Louise Lindner, was from the Shaker Heights family that was part of the Sterling Lindner department store. The Monday night show sold out in short order, but there was a bit of a problem getting the McCartneys to the Coliseum. The band flew in a chartered luxury jet that landed on time at Burke Lakefront Airport. The problem was, it was supposed to land at Cleveland Hopkins International Airport, so the plane took a short hop to the right place.

The show was set to begin at 8 p.m. and the doors opened at 7:30, but the crowds were so large that the concert was delayed for a few minutes to get people in the hall. Dick Wooten reviewed the concert for the *Cleveland Press* and reported the Coliseum staff treated the crowd "as if it were cattle. The experience was totally unpleasant." At about 8:40 the lights dimmed and McCartney and Wings took the stage. There was heavy fog on stage from dry ice machines, and even heavier fog from marijuana smoke in the audience. Wooten reported "the hard-edged music had a headlong and bloodthirsty brutality." That may be a little heavy-handed, but the volume was certainly distorted for at least the first few songs. Linda McCartney made a few references to Cleveland and Ohio State, Paul played new stuff and Beatle tunes, and the crowd loved it. They ended the show with an unreleased song called "Soily" and McCartney said the concert went so well the tune they played that night could end up on a live LP.

The Led Zeppelin shows the following April stand out for a number of reasons. The band always drew a loud and raucous crowd. A crush at the door left broken glass everywhere and featured more than a few arrests and a crowd screaming for the band long before it hit the stage. Zeppelin walked out to a two-minute standing ovation before they played a note. The volume was overwhelming but the fans didn't seem to mind, and huge silver beams of light washed over the crowd during "Stairway to Heaven." The band thought the shows went pretty well, too, and tour manager Richard Cole gave tapes of the Coliseum shows to the Zep fan club, issued as a three-record boxed set to members only.

The Who that played the Coliseum in December 1979 was far different from the band that had played there in 1975. Keith Moon had died the year before and had been replaced by former Faces drummer Kenney Jones. Jones was a very competent drummer, but who could replace Moon?

Then, three days before the Richfield show, the unspeakable happened when 11 people died and dozens more were injured in a stampede for seats at Cincinnati's Riverfront Coliseum. This brought back memories of the Led Zeppelin show in Richfield just a couple of years before, and the crowd for this Dec. 6 concert seemed fairly reserved. Before the concert began, Coliseum president Stuart Geller walked out in a three-piece suit to convey the Who's feelings about the Cincinnati event earlier that week. He told the crowd, "We couldn't let the night pass without taking a moment to recall the recent tragedy in Cincinnati. That we, like the entire entertainment industry, are shocked to think that something so devastating could happen to eleven young people. We don't intend to ever let it happen here." After a big response from the crowd it was time for the Who.

It took a little time for the band to interact with the audience, but once the show was underway everyone relaxed a bit. Pete Townshend thanked Geller and stressed how much the band loved Cleveland and the many friends they had there, "like the James Gang, and that's no bullshit." Oddly enough, the concert also included a clip from the film *Quadrophenia* that showed a riot and stampede from the band's early history in England. The Who would come back three years later for two shows that were expected to be their final U.S. concerts. The opening act on that tour was Little Steven Van Zandt and his Disciples of Soul. Among those enjoying the Richfield shows was the front man for Van

Zandt's other band, Bruce Springsteen, who watched from the side of the stage. He was a favorite at the Coliseum as well.

Bruce Springsteen and the E Street Band could fill stadiums, but they were no strangers to the "big house on the prairie." The Boss played the Coliseum several times, and the two-night stand that welcomed the year 1979 had the potential for disaster. Bruce and the band were played on every rock station but were linked to WMMS in the public eye. The station jumped on the Springsteen bandwagon early and benefited greatly over the years. When Springsteen agreed to play the Coliseum on New Year's Eve and the station announced it, the following day the tickets were snapped up in record time. This promised to be a party like no other.

David Lifton tells the story on the Ultimate Classic Rock website. Springsteen and company were riding the crest of the *Darkness on the Edge of Town* LP. The tour would come to a finale in Northeast Ohio. A few months before, Springsteen had played the Cleveland Agora in a radio simulcast to cities across the country, leaving local fans starving for more. Not long after was the two-night crossover with Southside Johnny, and that still wasn't enough. These final two shows of the tour were a "thank you" for the fans. Some just had a weird way of saying "you're welcome."

As usual, the band was really cooking that night and the crowd was pumped. At midnight there was a sing-along with "Auld Lang Syne," and then Springsteen and the boys tore into "Good Rockin' Tonight." This is where it got scary. Whoever it was might have been drunk, stupid, or both, but someone threw a lit firecracker that exploded near Springsteen's face. There was a cut under the right eye that got bandaged up, but you could tell by his language that "Miami Steve" Van Zandt was super-pissed. Springsteen was a bit calmer and grabbed a mic. The Ultimate Classic Rock site quotes him as saying, "I asked everybody, as I've seen people hurt at shows with firecrackers before, you know. I'm gonna ask you again because we're gonna be here tomorrow night . . . and you guys have always been great in this town. I love coming here and we love playing here—that's why we came on New Year's Eve.

And the only thing I ask is that people don't do stuff to hurt other people and to hurt themselves and to hurt me and whoever else is up here, because we came here to play some rock 'n' roll for you, and you guys paid your money so you . . . could listen without being afraid of getting hurt or blown up or whatever. So, if anybody sees anybody throwing stuff . . . just tell somebody so we can get 'em out. If you want to throw something, we'll give you your money back and you can throw it outside and do whatever you want."

Huge applause followed, and the show continued without incident, resulting in a bootleg that has been floating around for years. When Springsteen played Richfield in 1981, he came out dressed in jeans and a denim shirt while the rest of the band wore suits. That was the night of a famous duet with Southside Johnny. Springsteen returned the favor the next night. He also introduced a new song, "Johnny Bye Bye," which he dedicated to Elvis Presley.

The Rolling Stones were a touring machine, and Belkin Productions worked with tour coordinator Bill Graham to schedule two dates in November 1981. They had to work around other concerts, with the Stones road crew setting up the stage at 4 a.m. after a Foreigner/Billy Squier show the night before. The Belkins and Graham had great respect for each other, though Graham could be a bit testy. Belkin Productions booked three cities on that tour, including Buffalo and Syracuse. They spent $4,000 advertising the Buffalo show, and Graham snapped. Jules Belkin said, "Graham was furious! He said, 'Why are you spending money?'" Graham wanted to do the whole tour without spending a penny on promotion. Hey, it's the Stones! You didn't have to!

Big shows also cost a lot to produce, and no show was bigger than the Stones. Belkin used the Buffalo show as an example. Keep in mind these are 1981 dollars. "The stage rental is about $35,000. You pay 15-percent rent to the stadium owners. You pay insurance that comes to 12 cents a person (paid admission). There's about $35,000 for security. The catering backstage for three or four days can run up to $15,000. The sound and light will be about $25,000. Then you pay per diem on the road and pay for all those trucks."

Mileti's Monument: Rising from the surrounding fields like a Fortress of Solitude, Nick Mileti's Richfield Coliseum could be seen from far away as concert goers approached on the highways. *(Cleveland Press Collection, Cleveland State University Archives)*

For a lot of promoters that means you sweat it out until that last seat is sold.

The Stones' Richfield shows that Nov. 16 and 17 had blues belter Etta James as opening act, and started after 10 p.m., but no one seemed to care. They tore through their hits and Mick Jagger threw a bucket of water at the crowd. For the encore Jagger came out wearing a Cleveland Browns jersey with quarterback Brian Sipe's #17. Sipe was in the audience, a huge smile on his face.

So how did the Stones enjoy that first stop at the Coliseum? Bass player Bill Wyman called it "mediocre." He said, "The monitors weren't working right last night so we couldn't hear each other well enough onstage." It was a pretty sure bet that would be corrected for the second show. The second night came off a little better, though some crowd members caused a few problems, like tickets stolen out of people's hands, at least one assault on a police officer, and criminal trespass, but those incidents were quickly contained. Even so, some folks were not happy with all the attention being paid to the Rolling Stones.

A woman from Euclid wrote the *Plain Dealer* complaining,

"A group of sweaty, disgraceful men over the age of 30, jumping around on stage like they were being stung by bees. Why did they get so much attention?" She went on to write, "It's ridiculous to have wasted the tax-payers money when they were escorted from the airport by state highway patrol and deputy sheriffs with tight security. . . . Was there tight security when Slave, Cameo, Roger Troutman and Brick appeared at the Public Hall November 15?" Huh? Seriously? A reader from North Olmsted wrote that English rock critic Geoffrey Cannon described the Stones as "perverted, outrageous, violent, repulsive, ugly, tasteless, incoherent. A travesty. That's what's good about them" and "Birds of a feather flock together." Like that's a bad thing?

Some other Coliseum show highlights: Emerson, Lake & Palmer had an elephant on stage during "Karn Evil #9," U2's Bono and the Edge came out to play with David Bowie, and Eric Clapton had a living room set up on stage during his show.

Everyone has his or her favorite Coliseum memory, usually colored by some kind of mind-altering substance or experience. The Coliseum was open for business just shy of 20 years, but when Gund Arena opened in downtown Cleveland and the Cavaliers moved north, its days were over. There was talk about converting the building to a college, shopping center, or even a prison. Not to be. The walls came down in 1999, and today that site looks like it did in the early '70s—a big open space . . . with the ghosts of a lot of great memories.

Swingos'

HOTELS AND ROCK STARS have a long, twisted history. Debauchery reigned at the "Riot Hyatt" on Sunset Boulevard in Los Angeles, where Robert Plant stood on a balcony and screamed that he was a god. The Who are still under a lifetime ban from Holiday Inn after Keith Moon drove a Lincoln Continental into the swimming pool at the brand's Flint, Michigan, location. And New York City police dodged cherry bombs thrown at them from a window after—here's that name again—Keith Moon blew up the plumbing flushing explosives down the toilet at the Gorham Hotel. Just about every city has horror stories about rock stars, and very likely Moon, but everyone loved coming to Cleveland because of Swingos' Celebrity Hotel.

Jim Swingos and his family were entertainers in their own right. Artists came to town knowing the hotel had a top-rated restaurant, a superior wine list, exceptional security, and an owner who was very lenient as long as you paid your bills. They all paid, too—plenty, and word got around in the rock and roll community that Swingos' was a safe haven in a great market.

Swingos had been a well-known name on the local restaurant scene for years for the Keg and Quarter and got rave reviews when it moved into the Downtowner Motor Inn in 1967. The old restaurant operator owed $12,000, and that's what Swingos paid for the lease. The restaurant always drew, but hotels were suffering in the downtown area. Who would come to Cleveland, and why? When the opportunity arose in 1971, Swingos bought the hotel, renamed it, and started to refresh its 150 rooms into an oasis for visiting entertainers. People were still coming for the restaurant, but he had to get "heads in beds," and that was a pretty tough sell. Then he got a call from Memphis. Elvis Presley's tour was looking for a base of operations, something centrally located to travel to and from tour dates, with Cleveland as the hub. As the *Plain Dealer* reported, it was "One hundred rooms, three floors, and enough room service to keep the chefs working overtime—and Elvis had run up a $20,000 bill." And Presley loved the location. Reports say Presley's manager Colonel Tom Parker stopped in to check out the place on a Wednesday and Swingos had a special menu with fatback, corn bread, and collard greens. That scored some points, and the Colonel called Presley in a day early to see for himself. The paper also reported that Presley had certain demands. It quotes Swingos saying, "Elvis ordered a Boston strip steak and a chopped steak, a simple order. Then I took it up to the room and he says, 'OK, now cut it up into little pieces.' I did. Then he looks at 'em and says, 'Now, put 'em back together.'"

Presley's manager apparently took a liking to Swingos. One day they were sitting in the office talking about Presley's upcoming stay when the Colonel heard Swingos discussing terms for a show booking in the bar. Swingos later told a reporter, "Suddenly he cussed me out and told me to put the call on hold, which I did. He told me to insist on all the money up front for a week run with Jerry Lewis, Connie Stevens, and Pat Boone. I don't know why, but I did what he told me. I got the money up front. The show closed after three days. Ticket sales were zip after the third show. I don't know how he knew that. But he did."

The King was one story, but there also was the Chairman of the Board. When the Coliseum at Richfield opened in 1974, Nick Mileti booked rooms for Frank Sinatra and his entourage at Swingos'. This was a big deal, but "old Blue Eyes" was said to be very demanding. Swingos got on the phone with Sinatra's personal chef, found out that he loved fresh apple fritters and was a big fan of hot peppers. Swingos stocked his favorite dinner wine, Montrachet, and left plenty of lighters around in case he wanted

In addition to showing a very liberal attitude toward rock stars staying at his "celebrity hotel," Jim Swingos knew his way around a plate of peppers. Just ask Frank Sinatra! Here he serves customers at his Keg & Quarter restaurant in 1975. *(Cleveland Public Library)*

a smoke. On his first night, Sinatra sat down to dinner, Swingos sent over the peppers and stood out of sight to see if they passed muster. Reports say Sinatra tried one, threw down his fork and said, "Goddamn! These are the best peppers I ever had!" Giant sigh of relief!

Sinatra was in for another surprise.

On the day he checked out, Sinatra asked for the bill and Swingos said it was on the house. No way! Sinatra insisted he wanted to square up but Swingos wouldn't hear it. After a moment, Sinatra told Swingos to gather the hotel staff in the lobby, and then he went down the line with his bodyguard and handed each staffer a $100 bill. He told Swingos the hotel was like a new home, and he visited a number of times after that.

Many other artists were welcomed just as warmly, but they had bills to pay.

You can't ignore TVs dropping out of windows. Hey, someone has that room after you! A young Elton John reportedly ordered everything on the room service menu along with a number of bottles of expensive wine, took a nibble here and a sip there and then sent all of it out his window. Ian Hunter with Mott the Hoople was quoted as saying you remember checking in and out of Swingos' and nothing in between, and the Rolling Stones would spend an entire month taking up three floors satelliting out to various cities but always flying back to Cleveland. Now, those stories about Led Zeppelin.

When Zeppelin was at the Waldorf Astoria New York to be inducted into the Rock and Roll Hall of Fame in 1995, there was some lingering tension over the omission of bassist John Paul Jones from the Page-Plant tour. It was announced that there would be photos but no questions in the press room—as if that would stop anyone. When they took the stage, a shout rang out, "When are you coming back to finish the demolition work on Swingos'?" Jimmy Page turned with a big smile and proudly said, "Cleveland!" Zeppelin would use Swingos' as a tour hub, having a major, and often destructive, party just about every night. They went on in several rooms, and one guest once saw drummer John Bonham walk in and tear down two masts from a four-poster bed. He looked around with a shrug and said, "drumsticks." Very young girls and hangers-on were everywhere, each trying to outdo the other. Swingos recalled at the end of the tour he would walk from room to room with a tour accountant who clicked off damages on an adding machine. "How much for that bed?' "$2,000." "For a bed?" Swingos would say, "Industrial bed!" Never an argument. The accountant would total up thousands of dollars and ask, "Do you want that in cash, check or bank transfer?" They would make the transaction, shake hands, and it was "See you next tour!" Zeppelin had big fun, and Swingos got three floors of newly remodeled rooms.

Swingos also gave Bruce Springsteen a break on rooms early in his career when he couldn't afford $15 a night. They settled for $8 a room, and Springsteen always remembered that after his star rose dramatically. Not all rockers had such fond memories.

In a *Plain Dealer* story, Swingos recalled a fateful night saying, "I got a call at my house at 4 a.m. It was Yul Brynner complaining: 'This Deep Purple band is driving me crazy making noise.' So I showed up and saw Brynner going at it with Deep Purple guitarist Ritchie Blackmore." Swingos took a stand, saying, "I told that [expletive] Blackmore 'Can't you have some respect for Mr. Brynner?'" Blackmore is said to have called Brynner "a little French gypsy." They soon found themselves on separate floors.

Swingos' had such a stellar reputation that director Cameron Crowe not only insisted it be included in his film *Almost Famous* but demanded authenticity down to the pattern on the carpeting, which was only seen for a few moments in the film. Bette Midler also tipped her hat in one of her songs, though she mentions it was in Seven Hills. Hey, artistic license.

Swingos' didn't draw just rock stars. There were sports teams, actors, businessmen . . . lots of folks. You might even see Gene Simmons of Kiss with then-girlfriend Cher. But as a rule they didn't tear up rooms. Even so, all were welcome.

By the mid-'80s Swingos decided to move restaurant operations to the Statler Office Tower, and the old location became a Comfort Inn and later, dorms for Cleveland State University.

One last story before we turn the page on Swingos'. Record companies often held promotional parties at Swingos', which brought media people out in droves. One famous party had folks packed wall to wall, and a guy dressed as a policeman and mumbling incoherently handcuffed WMMS's Kid Leo to a young blonde. Then he left with the key! The fake cop? Who else? Keith Moon!

Gleason's Musical Bar

5219 Woodland Avenue, Cleveland

EVEN AFTER WORLD WAR II had ended, along with its patriotic fervor, Cleveland, along with the vast majority of the United States, had issues with racism, sexism, and antisemitism. White Christian guys had it made while everyone else struggled. Before freeways, most folks grew up and stayed in their own neighborhoods. Cleveland had its Little Italy and Little Warsaw, and other neighborhoods had their own ethnic identities. There was even a very small Chinatown. Segregation, common in the 1940s and '50s, helped spark the civil rights movement of the '60s and '70s. Along with social reformers, entertainers also helped break down walls.

Great music appealed to a wide and racially diverse audience, and Cleveland's Little Harlem, covering parts of Cedar and Quincy avenues, sections of Kinsman Road, and a long stretch of Woodland Avenue, was evidence of that. There were some amazing clubs: The Chatterbox, the Log Cabin, the Pla-Mor, Club Congo, Cedar Gardens, the Loop Lounge. Some tried promotions like the Wheel Lounge's "Surprise Night" on Wednesdays, where you could walk in and get fried chicken, hors d'oeuvres, or cheese sandwiches—but you didn't know which until you got there. Rip Bivins's Shangri La at Wade Park and East 79th Street had a "Champagne and Chitterlings" party. The Circle Theater had shake dancers between acts. Owners tried just about everything to get people through the door. But music was still the biggest draw, and in the very earliest days of rock and roll and Top 40 radio, Gleason's Musical Bar at East 55th and Woodland seemed to make history every week.

"The House that Jap Built" was the brainchild of William "Jap"

Gleason who, along with his manager Al Howell, started booking acts in 1942. It was a small place, seating maybe a hundred, and there was a dress code if you wanted to see the shows. Most of the early acts were black artists traveling the Chitlin' Circuit, playing to urban audiences eager for that kind of entertainment. Acts like Choker Campbell (who would go on to be an arranger and bandleader for Motown) and his Bachelors of Rhythm, Candy Johnson and his Peppermint Sticks, and others packed them into Gleason's every week.

Gleason's also had a first-class staff to serve the crowds.

The reason would seem obvious. Then, like today, if you depend on gratuities for a good part of your income, you try to give customers what they want for the tips that you need. The *Call & Post* newspaper profiled waitresses at a few of the inner city's best-known venues and found them to be "understanding and pleasant women" with a "broad understanding of human natures . . . forbearance and patience or she will not succeed at her job." Then there were the patrons who came in "to eat or drink with all their grudges with them." They could be a challenge. The writer spoke to Miss Lucille Callans at Gleason's, who tended bar during the day. "An even disposition helps even when you have to try really hard," she said she found over a year on the job. "If you can remain calm you'll find that you can handle almost anything that comes up." What came up on a weekly basis was great entertainment.

Often you had to have a gimmick, something to make people want to see you and get them talking to their friends. Bass Ashford knew that. When he and his trio got booked at Gleason's they gave folks plenty to talk about. Described as "sleek haired" and "amusing," Ashford was known for his "antics" on the bass fiddle. He worked the room, "always moving, always clowning" and playing his big fiddle to make it talk. When Decca Records sent the man described as a clean-cut Eddie Chamblee and his "upper crust music makers" it was a guaranteed packed room because his trumpet player, Pee Wee Jackson, was a Clevelander who used to live on East 144th. He said goodbye to his mom, Louise Franklin, in 1936 to cut his chops with top names including Fletcher Henderson, Jimmie Lunceford, and Earl Hines before he signed on with Chamblee. Hometown heroes put people in seats.

The club's reputation spread far and wide, and for many it was the only place people could see their favorite performers. Plenty of black music fans in outlying areas would travel to Cleveland to check out their favorites, but sometimes the locals would look down at them. At each table were souvenir paper hats, and if you put them on during the show the locals would single you out as being "country."

Alcohol and a bad attitude don't mix well, but Gleason's didn't see a lot of trouble. The key words here are "a lot." There was one incident in September 1951 when a patron said he was humiliated and embarrassed when he got roughed up by a manager outside the club. Now keep in mind, a buck was worth a lot more back then. The alleged victim filed suit claiming he was the target of loud and abusive language that embarrassed and humiliated him. Not only that, he claimed the manager held his shoulders, twisted him, and threw him sidewise and forward. That left him "sick, sore and lame" and he lost $11.79 when he couldn't work. All told, he estimated he was damaged to the tune of $6,511.79 but what the heck, round it off to $10,000. No word how that case was resolved.

People still came out to see the big acts, and the big acts kept on coming. Dizzy Gillespie, described as "the first disciple of Be-Bop," brought Joe Morris and his Applejackers, Doctor Stringbean, and "Crying Tommy" Brown to Gleason's.

It should be stressed that the color of money is green, and Gleason's welcomed both black and white audiences. A familiar face there was Alan Freed, who often played records by those entertainers on his WJW *Moondog Show* as rock and roll artists. In fact, Paul Williams and the Hucklebuckers and Tiny Grimes—who had "an art and a heart"—were favorites at Gleason's before Freed booked them for his infamous Moondog Coronation Ball on March 21, 1952. He also helped Gleason's regular Faye Adams, who sang with the Joe Morris Orchestra, to have solo hits with "I'll Be True

Gleason's Musical Bar offered major R&B talent of the day, including many performers who were just starting out on long careers.

to You" and "Shake a Hand." But some other performers helped fill the club, too.

In April 1953 the Cleveland Indians were red-hot and people stuck around after games to hit the town's night spots. When the Tribe opened its home season that year against the Chicago White Sox, the money flowed freely after the game at the Log Cabin, the Chatterbox, Club Trinidad, Gleason's, and just about any place with a liquor license. That August, Gleason's booked an act whose song "It Should've Been Me" had swept through Northeast Ohio like "fire through a lake of gasoline . . . and high test gasoline at that." It was Ray Charles and his orchestra, which packed every club they played in; even big names like Bullmoose Jackson and Charley "Good Time" Brown had a hard time getting the patrons to stop talking about the Charles revue. Charles got booked at Gleason's on a regular basis. When his hit "Drown in My Own Tears" was on the charts, Charles drew SRO crowds for a solid two weeks. Television was already starting to show up in the nation's homes, and Charles was proud to tell the audience he got screen time at a "video station" in Seattle.

Within the next few months the bar welcomed acts that the *Call & Post* described as "the throbbing kind of stuff that sets feet a-dancing," though Gleason's didn't have a dance floor. Eddie "Cleanhead" Vinson and the Cootie Williams Orchestra were favorites. So was Milt Buckner, the "Wild Man of the Hammond Organ," and when Fats Domino came to town promoting "Going Home" and "I've Got a Woman" the line went out the door. Blues great John Lee Hooker and his combo, along with Johnny "Guitar" Watson brought in huge crowds. Undiscovered local talent could pack the house, too.

Neighborhood bars and nightclubs—just about any place with a stage—gave local talent a chance. Babe Brondfield's Club Congo down the street hosted "Talent Night at the Congo," and there were plenty more opportunities to show your stuff. Jap Gleason had a "Fame and Fortune Night" every Monday and Tuesday with the finals on Friday. The clubs cooperated and even shared judges, with *Call & Post* writer John E. Fuster and WSRS-FM "disc jockeyette" Juanita "Sugar Lump" Hayes doing double duty at the Congo and Gleason's. Fuster was a big proponent of Cleveland talent, and was part of a group called the Starmakers Club. Another was promoter and raconteur Sid Friedman, who could put acts on the road if they showed they had the stuff.

It was common in those days to hire artists to work an eight-hour day. When they weren't on stage they helped get the club ready for the show that night. James Brown was known to haul beer at Gleason's when he wasn't belting out the tunes.

Back in those days people looked out for each other, and at Gleason's that applied to folks on both sides of the cash register. A benefit was held there in 1957 to help out barmaid Pauletta Johnson, who was battling tuberculosis. She'd been at Sunny Acres Hospital for a long time even though doctors believed she would recover completely and would be able to go home soon. Johnson had big plans before the illness, working at Gleason's, Café Society, and the Ebony Lounge to save money for a beauty course. But the disease wasn't on the same schedule as the doctors', and Johnson's funding was running out fast. Manager Al Howell put out the call and lined up an all-star cast for a Sunday benefit. On the bill were Willis "Gator Tail" Jackson and his orchestra, the Metrotones, comedian Tommy Patterson, Stella "Caledonia" Young, Billy Nightengale, and dancers Vickie and "Shaky Baby." That was a lot of entertainment for a three-hour show, only a dollar at the door. Howell even arranged for a telephone-loudspeaker hookup with Johnson from her hospital room.

The legends of American blues made Gleason's a "must" stop on any tour. Muddy Waters was one of the top touring acts when he arrived in March 1957. Strange as it seems, there were critics who predicted the blues was on its way out, but the *Call & Post* critic said they should "beg to be unquoted after they have heard Waters." Little Walter and his harmonica, Clifton Chenier and his blue accordion, and the Bobby Bland Orchestra with vocalist Little Junior Parker and Joe "Papoose" Fritz on alto sax, an act that charged top dollar, were huge draws. Reviews say Parker and Bland played to "a room so crowded that it seemed like the old wartime days" and predicted thousands of Clevelanders would see them before they left town for the next gig. That next year saw one of the hottest properties in show business, young sensation Jackie Wilson, settle in for a three-night stay. Wilson had been getting a lot of radio and TV for his hit, "To Be Loved," and was riding a wave of popularity. Blues belter Big Maybelle, who had shared a bill with Wilson at New York's Apollo Theater, said "I've never seen anything like him. He has everything that Sammy Davis and Elvis Presley have all rolled into one. He's a regular bombshell and a workhorse, too." She also said he had "the looks, the sex, the salesmanship to make him one of the very best."

Maybelle was big all right, at more than 250 pounds, but she also was a major talent. Before one 10-day stand at Gleason's she was hailed as "the greatest lady of lament since the late great Bessie Smith" and "is without a doubt one of the most magnetic personalities to play a Cleveland theater or nightclub during the past five years." Maybelle was known as a "stroller." She left the bandstand to walk among the patrons, running "through a room full of people like the warm rush of a spring breeze melting the icy leftovers of a hard winter." The newspaper critic stated, "She melts the hearts of even a Cleveland audience . . . and that, my friend, is a hard thing to do." As you can probably tell, Cleveland winters haven't changed that much over the years.

She was followed some time later by another "big" entertainer, "the Boss of the Blues," Big Joe Turner. Another heavyset blues belter at 250 pounds and 6 feet 2 inches, Turner didn't need a microphone and moved gracefully across the stage. A club performer going back to his days at the Backbiters Club in Kansas City, Missouri, where the owner wore high-button shoes and a $20 gold piece on his watch chain, Turner was 14 when he started but quickly won an audience for belting out blues with double-entendre lyrics. The owner of Kansas City's Kingfish Club would sneak him in and out the back door of his speakeasy so juvenile authorities wouldn't bust him.

This was a golden age of Cleveland R&B, a simpler and, in some cases, a more naïve period in city history. A bald female headliner named—this is not a joke—Jewel Brynner was told to shave her head to improve her vocal delivery. She toured with Little Walkin' Willie and his band. Alan Freed had long moved on to New York, but other white disc jockeys, like Bill Randle at WERE-AM and Sam "Crazy Man Crazy" Sampson at WSRS-FM, were still keeping an ear on the Woodland Avenue music scene. Sampson also owned the Hounddog's Den on East 116th, and he tried to one-up both Randle and Gleason's by booking the local debuts of Lazy Lester and Lightnin' Slim, with their respective hits "I'm Leaving You, Baby" and "Feelin' Awful Lonesome and Blue." It was the first appearance for both north of the Mason-Dixon Line.

There was plenty of competition, but Gleason's had the reputation and top artists were commonplace there into the early 1960s. The club business is a tough one, though, and even Gleason's had a shelf life. By 1962 the big Motown shows had started touring the country, offering a whole bill of acts for one price. Jap Gleason saw the writing on the wall and closed that same year. He went into real estate and died in 1996.

The legacy of Gleason's—which some might consider a footnote in Cleveland rock and roll history—lives on in a resting place a few miles east in Maple Heights.

Big Maybelle Smith had a short but prominent career. Legend has it that Billie Holiday marveled at her talent, and like Lady Day, Maybelle endured hardships into the 1960s. Her recording career faltered, and Maybelle even tried her hand at pop with remakes of Question Mark and the Mysterians' "96 Tears" and Donovan's "Mellow Yellow." She reportedly had a drug problem and returned to Cleveland to live with her mother. On top of that, she had advanced diabetes, and by 1970 her career was over. In January 1972, Big Maybelle was admitted to Cleveland Metro General Hospital, where she lapsed into a diabetic coma and died on the 23rd of that month. Finding a cemetery was difficult, but a small Jewish burial ground, Evergreen Cemetery at Rockside and Northfield Roads in Maple Heights, accepted her remains and now plays host on a regular basis to blues enthusiasts who travel there to pay their respects.

The Agora

2175 Cornell Road, Cleveland (1966–67)
1730 East 24th Street, Cleveland (1968–1984)
5000 Euclid Avenue, Cleveland (1985–)

NIGHTCLUBS ARE A TOUGH business. The hottest club in town can be packed one day and empty a few weeks later. Remember Nite Moves on Playhouse Square? The Mad Hatter? How about the House of Bud? There were days you couldn't get in the door, and now they're just footnotes in history. But one is still going strong after a half-century: the Cleveland Agora. The Agora story centers on Henry J. LoConti, who died in 2014. He had plenty of friends, and they all called him Hank.

He was born near East 12th Street and Scovill Avenue, where his parents had a grocery and butcher shop. LoConti started out as a kid unloading vegetable trucks for 50 cents apiece at the Orange Avenue farmers market. After graduating from John Hay High School and attending Kent State University, LoConti started a business servicing jukeboxes and vending machines. He had a good ear for music and would say that records by Johnnie Ray, Patti Page, and Tony Bennett showed him his future path. LoConti spent two years in the Army in Korea and came home to help run Club 18, the bar his family owned on Payne Avenue. Rumor has it that Elvis Presley stopped in around the time he was playing the Arena. That wouldn't be the last time LoConti hosted a major star at his place.

After the Korean conflict, it was back to jukeboxes for a time, and by the late 1950s LoConti had started a business with his brother supplying food for vending machines. They sold the company in 1963, and three years later LoConti opened the first

Hank LoConti's Agora drew crowds most nights of the week for major names and local talent. The club near the Cleveland State campus had people waiting in all types of weather for a shot at a prime seat near the stage. Here, fans line up for Southside Johnny in 1977. *(Janet Macoska)*

Agora in the old RIPA Hall on Cornell Road near the Case Institute of Technology campus. It was a private club for college students and their guests. You paid for a membership and got a photo ID; it cost 50 cents a visit, and your guests were a buck each. LoConti once likened it to the modern version of a malt shop, but instead of milkshakes it served 3.2 beer and there were even pewter mugs with members' names on them. It was a gamble. LoConti sank $20,000 into converting the old hall to a club, about what you would pay to build a new house back then. He started booking bands, but the noise didn't exactly endear him to the neighbors. The club started to generate complaints from nearby Little Italy, where people you didn't want to anger lived.

LoConti recalled other stumbling blocks. "When I opened up there at Cornell, it was February 1966, but we didn't get our license until November! We got so jam-packed in November, right after

Thanksgiving, I went looking for a new place downtown. I opened downtown in May, so I was only working there with a real license for about six months. The place was too small and the neighborhood was not exactly conducive to our business."

There was another major consideration. College crowds loved a good time and weren't afraid to spend money. "Remember, when I opened there, Case and Western Reserve University were separate. Female and male students. I still have the two membership cards saying Case Tech and Western Reserve. But our best customers were from John Carroll University. They could really put the beer away!" LoConti found a place on East 24th near Cleveland State University. Buddy Maver is one of the handful of people who know the inside story of the Agora. He'd known LoConti for years through playing with bands like Charade and Rainbow Canyon, and when LoConti offered him a position booking acts he signed on quick.

"The original building on East 24th Street was the best," Maver says. "It originally was a Clark's restaurant commissary. Clark's was a big chain in Cleveland. The front door of the Agora, that big metal door, used to be the loading dock. We built steps into the lobby, and when they tore down the Hippodrome, Hank bought these two showcases that were in the lobby where they would advertise coming attractions. That's where we put our upcoming shows. The traffic pattern was, if you went to the right you went to the bar, straight ahead was the VIP section, and to the left was the main room. Then [there was] the smaller room with the pool tables and, for a while, the mechanical bull."

The opening day was July 7, 1967, and the first band to play was the Selective Service.

LoConti also opened a Columbus Agora to serve the Ohio State crowd.

Columbus turned into a good town for LoConti, with plenty of memories. There was a night when, he recalled, Alice Cooper was ripping open feather pillows. Feathers everywhere got sucked into the overhead exhaust fan. "About two weeks later, we're not getting any air in the auditorium. I called this old man in, and he looks it over in the basement. He checked it out and said, 'No problem! Someone reversed your polarity.' Ted Nugent was on stage at the time, and the old guy turned on the system and said, 'Now it's working!' All of a sudden, my manager comes running downstairs and said, 'You won't believe what's happening!' Feathers all over the club. Nugent thought it was great!"

The new Cleveland location was not easy to find. But if you give people a reason to come they'll find you, and LoConti started booking some of the area's better-known bands. Along with Charade, you had the Sensations on Wednesdays, Joey and the Continentals on Fridays, and the Originals on Sundays. The James Gang played the downstairs bar the Mistake before anyone knew who they were. The first nationally known band LoConti booked was The Buckinghams, and he knew he was onto something good. Word got around, and it wasn't long before folks started coming in from the suburbs.

By 1970, Cleveland had two progressive rock FM stations, WNCR and WMMS. They didn't sell a lot of commercial time, pushed the envelope with their on-air programming, and had the same target demographic LoConti wanted walking through his door. An alliance formed. He started broadcasting live shows.

"We actually started live broadcasts from our club in Columbus on WNCI-FM. We did our first broadcast in June 1970 with Ted Nugent. We thought it worked out well so we would tape the show on WNCI, and send it to Cleveland to sister station WNCR. That went on from June 1970 to the time I came back to Cleveland in August '71. In the new place in 1971 we had the recording studios attached to the club so we went live in Cleveland and shipped the tape down to Columbus. We did that for about a year until we stopped doing them live. To make things easier we would record the shows on Wednesdays and put it on both WNCR and WNCI. It eventually grew to the point where we had nine stations."

Even so, the broadcasts could be challenging. "When we did them live, timing was critical," LoConti recalled. "We had to start the show at exactly 10 o'clock, run it for exactly an hour, and then cut it off. It also meant that the show never had a finale. That was usually toward the end of the show, but there was no set time. When we recorded the show we could edit an hour-and-a-half show down to 58 minutes."

He also learned just how volatile the radio business could be.

"FM was a baby, but it grew rapidly. WNCR and WMMS were the two that really built the FM radio scene in this town. Unfortunately, WNCR decided at the end of 1972 that it didn't fit the image of the parent company, Nationwide Insurance. A memo came down that all their stations were going to change their formats. I remember getting a phone call from a WNCI manager in Columbus, and he said, 'Hank, get off of us.' Get off of us? What's that supposed to mean? 'It means we're changing our formats. Columbus, Cleveland, and across the country.' Meanwhile, the guy with the same job in Cleveland is saying, 'No, no! Rock and roll 'til we die!' What's the story here?"

LoConti did a bit more detective work. "I called back to Columbus, it's late October, and that same guy at WNCI says, 'I'm telling you, I have the memo in front of me. We're changing!' Carl Hirsch at WMMS used to come to have lunch at the Agora, and every time he stopped in he would say, 'Hank, you gotta give me that live concert show.' Same answer all the time. 'Carl, I can't. I've got two stations and I have to feed Columbus.' This time it was different. I called him up and said, 'Carl, I'm going to give you the show', but he wanted it the next week. Can't do that. It had to wait until the first of the year 1973. I wanted to book a bunch of strong shows, and we lined up 13 of them, one a week starting the first week of January. Incredible shows! Two dollars at the door to see Bob Seger open for Ted Nugent, Robin Trower opening for Peter Frampton, one of the earliest shows of Bachman-Turner Overdrive, and Bad Company's first show in the U.S. Thirteen great weeks!"

The Who never played the Agora, but they did make an appearance there. As a favor to another promoter, LoConti offered to pick up the band at Burke Lakefront Airport. Maver says, "Hank picked them up and took them to Captain Frank's and it was closed. Keith Moon jumped in Lake Erie! They fished him out and Hank said, 'I'll take you back to the Agora' and I'll make you some burgers." The lake was not nearly as clean as it is now, so whatever soaked into Moon's clothes stunk to high heaven—and the aroma lingered in LoConti's car. The Who also had an after party at the Agora following its August 12th, 1971 show at Public Hall.

The WMMS connection proved critical. According to Maver, "My mission was to not lose money. The Agora was doing great business five nights a week. Wednesday through Sunday. booking local dance bands. We were dark Monday and Tuesday, and I had to fill those two nights with something to draw people and make money.

"We made a deal with WMMS to be the station to present all of our concerts. We couldn't afford to buy spots because of the ad rates. But according to the FCC they could air promos, so our deal was once each time segment they would read our laundry list of nights out at the Agora, the upcoming shows, and maybe give offhand comments if they played a record by the artist that was coming in. If the show wasn't selling we would do a ticket giveaway, which was another free mention. We also did quite a few $1.01 shows where the record company would get behind an act. We did U2 for $1.01. The record company would pay our production expenses . . . lights, sound, catering, stage crew . . . and the company would then get the gate. These kinds of shows only happened if WMMS was really behind the record in hot rotation. Great way to break an unknown act. The fans thought if WMMS put its stamp on it, the act must be good." But everyone benefited with this deal. As Maver puts it, "WMMS needed us and we needed them. They needed us because we became a physical location for them. Their logo was all over the club. We always had a WMMS DJ hosting the show." Lots of people saw those logos, too, but you still had to have a draw.

LoConti told the same tale. "We had Bob Seger open for Ted Nugent, and the reason was we could never draw a crowd with him, and we played Bob Seger from 1970 until he finally made it in '74 or '75. At this particular time he had just come out with a new album, and his agent told me it was the hottest thing he had ever done. We sold 51 tickets. It's 1 o'clock in the afternoon on the day of the show and Joyce Halasa and I were talking. We had to do something! I thought if we could get the record company to pay the act, we'd pay for the production and give the show away for free. Called the agent, called John Gorman at WMMS, and everybody said okay. A free show from the record company and 'MMS. By the time we had all this done, it was 4 or 4:30. I would also go over to the Cinnamon Bear to eat before a show. I put on the radio in the car at 5 o'clock and they're already blasting away about the show. You can't do that today. You can't call a radio station and do that today. It's impossible. I had 1,100 people there that night."

More than once the club stumbled into history. Bad Company made its U.S. debut on the Agora stage in 1974, and there were plenty of similar gems, but Maver says booking shows took a lot of patience and a lot of time.

"We got on a plane to New York and met all the agents at Premiere Talent, ATL, William Morris, ICM, and a couple of the others," Maver says. "About six agencies handled ninety percent of the bookings. I came back to Cleveland and my first office was right in the lobby at the Agora. It was convenient because when I was covering a show it was a great getaway from the 'maddening crowd.' My life for the next six years was spent on the phone eight hours a day. From 1976 to '82 I only went to lunch one time. I had to work through lunch because for every call I had there were two on hold, because all the smaller agencies like DMA in Detroit and Monterey Peninsula Artists on the west coast were pitching acts to me. It was easy to pick the headliners we knew would sell tickets, but it was tough to pick the 'baby' acts when you didn't know how well they were going to do."

There was pressure, too, and sometimes you just had to trust people.

"Sometimes if a manager had 'juice' they would say, 'I want you

Hank LoConti (shown here in 1976) built the Agora from a single night club near Little Italy to a chain of clubs stretching all the way to Texas. *(Cleveland Public Library)*

to help me with this baby act and I'll give you a bigger name.' But a lot of time that came from agents. They would twist my arms, but that power shifted when we opened other Agoras because I could book five-six dates. Cleveland, Columbus, Toledo, and Youngstown. We could give them four dates in Ohio, and then we opened in Atlanta in '78, near Miami and in Tampa, and Dallas and Houston. I could do 10 dates if the routing was there, and at the club level they didn't fly. They drove. You couldn't have too long of a drive between dates."

By 1977, the Agora was bringing in as much as $4 million a year, but it also had plenty of expenses to deal with. LoConti told reporter Scott Eyman, "Our money, our profit, basically comes from the cover charge; the music generally has a high overhead and we don't make it at the bars because we don't hustle drinks. We don't have table service and we don't even have stools at the bars. You've really got to want a drink to get one, and that's the way I want it; I'm not in the bar business. I'm in the music business." There's a lot to be said for that statement. At one point the Agora had automated drink mixers. It poured the exact amount of alcohol every time, and a lot of people didn't like what they were getting. LoConti also wanted a quality shop to visit and play in. "I put cedar on my walls. I run a clean place. I put in dishwashers at all bars, because after you wash a dozen beer glasses in a sink you're not washing in soap, you're washing in beer. And the music. If you played the Agora you were at least decent and you got paid. You weren't just a bunch of stiffs."

LoConti didn't care for a lot of the music he booked; his tastes ran from Melissa Manchester and Olivia Newton-John to the softer stuff on radio. Plus, new bands were often touring on a shoestring, but if they had promise, they got booked. For example, Maver recalls, "When the Police first came out they rolled up in a van. We asked, 'Where's your equipment truck?' and they said, 'This is it!' The Police was a family affair. The drummer was Stewart Copeland, and their agent was his brother, Ian, and his other brother Miles owned the record label IRS. The Police played the Cleveland area so often when they were starting out that some thought they were a local band."

Of course, not every act was a draw.

Chuck Zingale was LoConti's brother-in-law and ran the Plato and the Mistake. He'll tell you, "I had Tiny Tim at the Plato. Horrible. He drew 28 people. It was after he had been on a TV talk show and he said something bad about college kids . . . and we had a college club!" Word got around if an act didn't like the audience.

Other than the bands, how did LoConti get people to the clubs? Some of it was word-of-mouth, and there was advertising on radio and in *Scene*, but some of it was guerrilla marketing. He once dis-

tributed hundreds of free tickets at an all-female college knowing
that would likely bring in hundreds of guys. In mid-1978 the club
also did a makeover and installed a computerized dance floor with
Wally Bryson's Fotomaker as opening-night band. The Agora even
kicked off its 12th anniversary with a dance team, the Agora Rock-
Ettes, and a special show by the Cars for $1.01 a ticket.

But the most famous show ever at the Agora didn't even cost
a dime.

It was August 9, 1978. LoConti remembered how it all came
together as if it were yesterday. "It was WMMS's 10th anniversary,
it was our 13th, and there are a whole lot of stories how it happened. 'MMS and I were both sort of told it was ours. I was in Los
Angeles at the time for Columbia Records' party for Meat Loaf. The
Meat Loaf album was the album of the year, and the Cleveland guy
for Columbia [Steve Popovich] was at the party. We were talking
about celebrating our 13th anniversary, and he said, 'It would be
great if we could get somebody from Columbia to play for you.
What do you think about Springsteen?' I said, 'Sure! I'd like to go
to the moon, too!' I thought he was kidding. Sure enough, they
put it together!"

Maver has plenty of memories of that show, too. "The record
company bought all the tickets at $7.50 apiece, which was a high
ticket price at that time. Our concerts were $4.50 to $5.50 for
anybody, and a buck more at the door. The company gave the
tickets away on 'MMS and there was a 10-city radio simulcast.
They brought in Jimmy Iovine to do the radio mix. In 1978 Iovine
was a young kid engineer, and not a big-time producer or label
owner at that time. They showed up in the afternoon to set up
and Bruce asked, 'Do you have any eight-foot tables?' The stage
crew found eight of them, and Bruce had us nail them to the stage
perpendicular, you know stage right, the middle, and stage left. He
used them as ramps, and at certain points during the show Bruce
would give a nod to Clarence Clemons and Miami Steve and walk
out in the audience."

It turned into one of those shows that everyone remembers

attending. (Sort of like David Bowie's U.S. debut at Cleveland Music Hall in 1972: 3,000 tickets sold, and 20,000 people say they were there.) LoConti recalled, "Anybody that was anybody in Cleveland was at that show. I remember seeing the Browns' quarterback Brian Sipe in the audience." The tour de force performance became the most heavily bootlegged show ever. (It was finally officially released by the Springsteen camp in 2015.)

Just a few weeks later, Springsteen was booked at the Richfield Coliseum and his old buddies Southside Johnny & the Asbury Jukes were set to play the Agora. It was a pretty safe bet they would meet up at some point, and Southside did a walk-on at the Coliseum. LoConti also had a five-camera video crew shoot to include Southside Johnny on the *Live at the Agora* TV series to be taped that same evening.

As LoConti recalled, "Southside called us from the Coliseum. We had Wild Horses playing, and then Southside was supposed to come on. He called and said, 'We're going to be late. Can you hold the show?' Sure. He said, 'Springsteen wants us to jump on the stage with him.' Wild Horses did another set, and Southside Johnny showed up and walked on stage. We got into the show, and the last 28 minutes I'll never forget. All of a sudden, here comes Miami Steve. Everybody's cheering, and then here comes Springsteen!"

Maver clearly remembers that night. "We were filming Southside Johnny for our TV show. We did about 10 shows for Channel 8, WJW-TV. We would film them live at the Agora, do some post production, and air on Channel 8 against *Saturday Night Live*. Some of those nights we beat them in the ratings. The audio was simulcast on WMMS.

"Bruce got done at the Coliseum and shows up at our back door, gets on stage with Southside for the last three songs. Everyone's show builds to a climax and your last three songs are your best songs. I'm watching and thinking 'Now this is a TV show!'"

So what happened to the tape? Couple of different opinions about that.

LoConti needed Springsteen's and Southside's okays, and he set up a meeting in New York with their management and showed the tape. He said Miami Steve turned thumbs down because Southside was a separate act. Plus, LoConti said, it was pointed out that Springsteen looked so thin! (Does that seem likely? Well, not long after, Bruce Springsteen looked like he did some quality time in a gym.)

Maver, though, has a different take on that meeting.

"The next day—Hank always said it was Miami Steve, but I heard it was Jon Landau, who was Bruce's manager, who nixed showing that footage because, at that time, Bruce had not done a video yet. He didn't want his first video to be this jam thing."

The show, sans Springsteen, was syndicated to a bunch of different markets around the country.

The Agora saw its share of unique personalities over the years both on and off the stage. Manny Iacano worked for LoConti for a time both in Columbus and Cleveland, and said one sure bet at the Cleveland location was seeing "Daffy Dan" Gray, the T-shirt king, at just about every show. "He was like a maître d' greeting you at the door whenever a band came through," according to Iacano, "usually with his dog." You always knew when Gray was on the scene before you even saw him. That was his car parked in the no-parking zone in front of the club. Certain perks come with being a club-hopper!

Gray says, "I was out every night from the time I could get out of the house. I saw the Yardbirds with Jeff Beck and Jimmy Page at the Mentor Hullaballoo. The Agora? Yeah, I was a fixture there. Never had to pay, either. Hank's sister-in-law took care of the box office so she would just wave me in. I was there just about every night, especially Monday night when the record companies would introduce their bands. They'd have a party downstairs before the show, you went upstairs to see the act and then back in the basement when it was over. Local bands during the week, and I was there for them, too. It was just part of the scene."

That's a key observation.

"The Agora was one of the key gathering places for the Cleveland-area music scene," Gray says. "It was the great equalizer. You could be the biggest nerd at your school or the most popular kid in your neighborhood. If you were part of that scene, you were okay. There was a constant flow of people, and they were as interesting as the bands. We don't have that anymore, except for the folks who were part of it back then getting together to see old bands or share memories. Back in those days when you saw somebody who was even a little older at a show you were like, 'Huh? What's he doing here?' Now we're older and say, 'Who are the kids?' That's why my business succeeded. I gave the kids in that scene their uniforms."

Those weren't his only memories.

"I remember the smell of stale beer and cigarettes. I didn't smoke but I always smelled like old cigarettes when I left the building.

"The Agora was a key element in that whole scene, but there were a lot of elements that all worked together. Great radio stations, concert promoters, the bands, and bars. The underground press. All the stars lined up in a row. If one of those elements was missing, the scene wouldn't have worked. No one had that environment anywhere else. Maybe San Francisco, but Cleveland by far was the best."

Things moved fast for LoConti and his crew. In its 13th year, the club formed its own record label and signed Artful Dodger as its first artist. There were even plans for a separate custom label called—get this—"Oh, Henry." Paul Simon also set up shop for a small hall concert and a movie shoot.

"Paul Simon did parts of *One Trick Pony* at the Agora," Maver says. "He was there for six weeks filming, and during that time I had the B-52s doing a show. He saw them and liked them and asked if we could get them back in two weeks to be in the movie. They were going to use my office as the set for the guy playing the club manager, and then they discovered the 'dungeon.' It was a sub-basement that was old and dingy, and that was the look they wanted." It's a rare chance to see a part of the Agora that people didn't know about.

The occasional headache would occur, and one in December 1979 turned into a major migraine.

It started on December 3. A couple of Fire Department lieutenants stopped in to check on possible overcrowding. They had to get past a security guard who was also an off-duty cop. The fire officials were not in uniform but showed their identification. Still, security wasn't about to let them just waltz in. What followed was described as a "conflict of authority," with the key word being conflict.

The cop was backed up by about 10 bouncers, and when the fire officials tried to push their way in, security pushed back. Hard. The truth is gray, but the guys from the fire department say they got badly roughed up, held in armlocks, pushed into an office and illegally detained for several hours. One of the folks at Agora Broadcasting, which taped the shows for syndication, later claimed the inspectors were, "immature, hostile and constantly shouted obscenities to people after barging into the place."

The fire marshals had the power to stop ticket sales, and they said the building was at capacity and no one else could be allowed into the hall. Both sides started throwing hands. At least one witness claimed an inspector threw the first punch, though another said the marshal was thrown against a wall first.

The Cleveland Fire Department argued it didn't need any paperwork to inspect a building during business hours. The question was, what exactly were the Agora's business hours?

Additional police and fire were both called, and the inspectors were freed after several hours. But it got messier after that. There were strained relations between city police and fire, the club was cited for overcrowding, and it didn't stop there.

Fire officials started researching the Agora's records at the building department and found it had never been issued a certificate of occupancy. The club also had been cited the previous May for not building a firewall between the first floor and the basement bar, the Mistake. That was followed by another fire inspection in January, and the Agora got busted for overcrowding. The legal capacity was said to be 684, and the inspectors counted over 1,000.

LoConti said the charge was a load of crap because the club could safely accommodate a thousand. Cleveland Municipal Court Judge Joseph McManamon didn't buy, and fined the club $100.

*   *   *

Punk rock never really took off in the U.S. like it did in England. British fans coupled music with fashion, and Cleveland was one of the few U.S. cities that had a small but enthusiastic punk community, due possibly to an unlikely source. Jimmy Zero of the Dead Boys said the generation that grew up in Cleveland watching Ernie Anderson's "Ghoulardi" character on late-night TV saw anarchy as entertainment. (Which is ironic because Anderson hated rock and roll—he was a jazz guy and even rejected an invitation to meet the Beatles in 1964.)

By mid-1980, punk probably was as big as it would get, and the Agora hosted punk rockers along with a lot of different types of music.

"The Sex Pistols wanted the Agora to be their first show in America," Maver says. "We booked them and it sold out in a day. It was supposed to be New Year's Day 1978. They were leaving Heathrow Airport to come to Cleveland the day before the show, and Johnny Rotten said something really nasty to the customs agent and they wouldn't let them leave the country. They got to America a day or two late but they missed our show. They rescheduled our show for the end of the tour, and during the tour the band broke up. They never made it to Cleveland."

"A year later, middle of May in 1980, we booked Johnny Rotten with Public Image Ltd. He came out in this checkered jacket and was egging on the audience. He turned his back on the crowd to get a drink of water and somebody spat a huge wad on the back of his jacket. It stayed there the whole show." The assistant manager at the Agora, David Dubs, said Lydon was a total professional. "He was easy to work with, right on time. No trouble at all." This also showed the difference between the various acts and audiences they drew to the club.

Cleveland's Fillmore: Established stars knew the Agora had a demanding audience that rivaled crowds and venues in any other major city. Todd Rundgren packed the room with his frequent stops at the club, this one from 1978. *(Janet Macoska)*

Punk audiences didn't want to follow rules like showing IDs, or stand in lines. They might've smoked some weed in the club, but if you were caught once you were told to put it out; twice and you were put out the door. They didn't buy drinks like country music audiences who knocked back whiskey, rock fans who drank beer, or jazz audiences into mixed drinks or wine. They behaved a lot differently, too. Bob Smith, a soundman, found that out the hard way when one of the punks bit him on the ankle when he was trying to adjust an amplifier on stage.

Wally Gunn was with a punk comedy band called the Baloney Heads. He remembers, "There was one time in the summer, I went every night for two weeks. How many clubs are open that way anymore with live music every night? Buddy Maver booked us to open for the Dead Boys on a Monday night. Prior to that the Rubber City Rebels had played and people had bombarded the stage with cans and bottles. The club wasn't happy about that.

Look, it was dangerous! Then we played and the same thing happened. When we finished, Hank came out, looked around and said, 'plastic cups only!'

"Punk audiences were good but back then it was almost a regular thing to throw stuff at any band that played. In England, they were spitting on people, so I was okay with cups flying. Buddy called me at my day job and asked if we could open the show. Didn't hesitate. 'Absolutely!' and I called the band to tell them we were opening the Monday night show. There were a lot of established bands that were not happy they were passed over."

The *PD*'s Jane Scott wrote that one band, the Rebels, told the audience they "couldn't hit the broadside of a barn" and that's when the drinks started flying.

One of the most-repeated Agora stories involves Elvis Costello, or, to be exact, his manager, Jake Rivera. Jane Scott was everyone's friend but she didn't like Rivera. Here's why. She said that after Costello's debut at the Agora, the press was led backstage and told not to speak. When Costello walked in, Scott said, "Hi, Elvis!" and Rivera let loose. Maver says, "He actually said, 'Get that fat old lady out!' I told Rivera, 'You can't talk to her like that! That's Jane Scott!' He was an asshole. I believe that he was trying to turn Elvis Costello into the angry young man. We almost came to fisticuffs over that backstage thing. He was downright nasty. At the time the punk thing was really big in Britain, and Elvis was not a punk. He was a melodic singer-songwriter, but Rivera tried to fashion him into the angry young man." Another story had Rivera wanting to face Maver in a pistol duel in a dispute over ticketing.

Punk may have been a niche audience, but country was getting bigger thanks in part to John Travolta's film *Urban Cowboy*. With LoConti's multiple Agora locations, there was plenty of potential for the country fans. That audience, with deep pockets when it came to the bar, was big enough that LoConti renamed the Painesville Agora the Urban Cowboy Saloon. Along with the bands, the crowning touch was the El Toro mechanical bull ride LoConti bought from Gilley's, the Texas honky-tonk where parts of the

Travolta movie were filmed. The bull didn't come cheap. LoConti paid $7,000, and then it was delayed for a week when it got lost in shipping. It cost an extra $700 to ship it by plane once they found the crate. The bull was mobile and would be shipped to the Cleveland Agora when a big country act was coming through. That's when WHK was a huge country radio station and supported country shows the same way sister station WMMS backed rock.

The Agora wasn't just about concerts. It also sponsored a "Love in the Afternoon Club" for soap opera fans, and an air guitar championship got ink in Tom Batiuk's *Funky Winkerbean* comic strip. One of the characters, Crazy Harry, showed up in the strip to compete, and Batiuk made an appearance that night to sign autographs at the event sponsored by WWWM-FM (M105).

LoConti demanded a lot from his staff, but most would say he gave as much as he took. Suzy Peters did promotions at the Agora. One day she walked into LoConti's office to ask for a raise. His desk was covered with pink "while you were out" slips. Peters says, "I asked Hank if we could talk, and he swept all the papers into a trash can. The desk was clear. I asked, 'Don't you need those?' and Hank said, 'If it's important. They'll call back. Right now, you're the most important!'"

A good part of the history of the Agora is linked to the WMMS Coffee Break Concerts. LoConti had plenty of fond memories. "Cyndi Lauper, John Mellencamp, Pat Benatar—they all played the Coffee Breaks. Bon Jovi was actually forced into playing a Coffee Break Concert. We had shows on Monday nights, and we finally had to do Mondays and Tuesdays. We were doing over a hundred shows a year. Sometimes we even did Sundays. We booked Bon Jovi for a Tuesday evening show, and he sold maybe 30 tickets. His manager at the time was Doc McGhee, and we decided we were going to cancel the show but put him on for free the next day. People that bought tickets would get their money refunded. Bon Jovi did the Coffee Break Concert that next day and wasn't sorry he did it." For many, the concerts were also like midweek vacations. "Our Coffee Breaks were packed every week no matter

Nights Out: The Agora had a long and successful run promoting shows with "The Buzzard," WMMS. This poster shows just some of the amazing array of talent that benefited from both heavy radio promotion and their stage time at the club.

who we played. People would start lining up at 10 in the morning and the show didn't start until noon." Oh, and the bar was open as soon as you walked in!

According to LoConti, "It was Denny Sanders's idea to start the Coffee Breaks. They did the first ones outside the station at a place called Bobby McGee's on 17th and Euclid Avenue. It was a little place. When they got there to set up equipment for the band, the place was closed. The manager had slept in and never showed up to open. I called Sanders and told him to do the shows at my place. We will be open! We made a deal to have it at the Agora, and we never closed. Open every single Wednesday, and if we didn't have a national act we played a local band. We never missed a Coffee Break Concert. We always had at least 800 people there and it didn't matter who was on stage. We could also get 1,500 to 1,600 people in there if we had to." There were plenty of times they needed that space, too.

By 1983 the Agora had a history few could even try to rival. Modern English played a Coffee Break Concert, "Weird Al" Yankovic appeared with Dr. Demento, and the shows kept coming. Maver remembers them well. "John Mellencamp played to about 50 people at the Agora. That was when he was known as John Cougar, and his manager was over by the bar griping about the turnout. Joe Cocker. Loved him, but he had a five-gallon bucket behind the amps backstage because he had to expel a few times during the show. Joe Perry from Aerosmith. When he played the Agora he was not in the shape he is in now. Kenny Loggins was booked at the last minute at the Akron Agora when a strike canceled his Blossom show. He packed the place, and at the end he said, 'You guys are great! I can't wait to come back'. As he was walking from the stage we asked if he really wanted to come back and he said, 'No.'"

Some of the acts left some weird memories.

"Lou Reed had it in his contract that he had to be picked up at the airport in a Town Car," Maver says. "That was somehow forgotten, but Hank LoConti had a big green Lincoln [so] Hank himself went to pick up Lou at the airport. Lou is there with this very striking transvestite. They get in the back seat of Hank's Lincoln, and they're heading to Swingos'. Hank's driving, and he looks in the rearview mirror to change lanes and Lou is having a little romance in the back seat! Hank didn't look back there again."

Others are memorable for other reasons.

"We did the first four shows that Meat Loaf ever played. He put so much into it that he collapsed backstage and we had to give him oxygen. He was a big guy. A few days later he's playing a sold-out show at the Painesville Agora and Tom Petty is the opening act. Onstage during the sound check Tom Petty is standing there smoking a cigarette. A thousand people can't come in yet because Petty is still doing his sound check. I went up to him and said, 'Hey, man. We have to open the doors because it's starting to rain.' He said, 'I'm not done yet!' I told him, 'Yes, you are' and we opened the doors. The next day I get a call from Premier Talent saying Tom wasn't happy about that.

"Some of the acts had cult followings. They didn't sell a lot of records, but guys like Leon Redbone would bring in 800 people. Rory Gallagher, Roy Buchanan, same thing. Didn't sell records but lots of tickets."

There was the occasional emergency.

"We booked the Clash just after their first album came out, and I got a call from their manager day of show saying Joe Strummer had a terrible toothache. I called up my dentist, Sid Foreman, and he fixed him up but he couldn't believe his teeth!"

The Agora kept plugging along with an occasional face-lift and lots of shows, but 1984 turned into a major turning point for the club. Cleveland State University wanted the land for physical education facilities. LoConti only leased the building, so the Agora would be looking for a new location. Then that October a CSU police officer spotted smoke coming from the Agora. The fire crew was on the scene in minutes. Fire had broken out near two gas air conditioners and spread to the ballroom. The skylights and ceiling caved in, and there was about $30,000 damage. Shows were canceled, and after a time it was decided the East 24th Street location was no more.

Everyone agreed the Agora was too important to die, and the search was on for a new venue.

It took a while and a lot of money, but LoConti settled on the old WHK Auditorium at 5000 Euclid. Over the years, the former Metropolitan Theater had been a vaudeville house, movie theater, and burlesque joint, and for a short time in the 1960s, Detroit promoter Russ Gibb operated it as the Grande Cleveland. Acts that played there included the Moody Blues in a show that doubled as a client party for WMMS, and a bizarre Halloween date in which Devo was chased off the stage. The show was recorded and released on CD as *Devo Live: The Mongoloid Years.* Try to find a copy now, and be ready to dig deep if you do.

The stage at the new Agora was bigger, there were 1,200 seats and a capacity of 1,500. Opening night was November 23rd, 1986 with a show featuring Ian Hunter from Mott the Hoople, former Spider from Mars Mick Ronson, and Jack Bruce of Cream. The new phase had begun.

Plenty of people who performed at the Agora have stories. Tommy Rich played drums for a load of bands, including American Noise and Donnie Iris & the Cruisers. Agora memories? Like you wouldn't believe! "I was a roadie for the band Ambleside before I ever played the Agora. At 15, I'm going to the Agora every Thursday night to set up gear for Circus. I didn't have a license yet, but I was driving their truck. When the band members weren't available, I took advantage of all the backstage 'fringe benefits and debaucheries' that a 15-year-old roadie could handle. That's when I thought I could probably do even better if I could play an instrument!"

Rich says his role in American Noise opened a lot of new doors. "We were still called 747 'cause we hadn't released our record yet, and we opened for Artful Dodger. Remember them? They were the biggest assholes in the world. They gave us two inches of room on the stage, and the drummer is standing on the side of the stage watching me play with his arms crossed. So I broke a stick and flung it. Hit him right in the forehead."

Rich says Agora concerts rank among his favorite memories. "I saw U2 at the Agora. There were 75 people there. I saw the Police at the Painesville Agora, XTC. The worst and the best were the Coffee Break Concerts. For a time they were at 11 a.m. American Noise were regulars on the Coffee Break Concerts, and for us to play with that intensity at that hour with a 9 a.m. sound check—well, you know what you had to do. You had to stay up all night. In those days we were doing enough blow to coat the North Pole.

Early exposure at the Agora helped set the Michael Stanley
Band on a record breaking run at much larger venues.

"My favorite backstage story was the American Noise record
release party. Sold out, broadcast live on WMMS. Murray Saul was
our promotion guy. He was the Elektra guy, and Planet Records
was part of Elektra. After the show we're going apeshit back there.
Murray is so fucked up and he turns around to this big industrial sink, pukes, rinses his mouth out with a drink, and carries on
drinking. Now, that was a manly man right there."

Dale Stradiot was the drummer for the band Jasper. They got
a lot of work at the Agora opening for the Police, Depeche Mode,
and Dolenz, Jones, Boyce & Hart, among others. You never knew
who might walk through the door.

"We were playing at the Agora one night," Stradiot says, "and
Gene Simmons and Paul Stanley of Kiss showed up. The Agora was
a proving ground. They were playing at the Richfield Coliseum on
Friday, Jasper was playing on a Thursday night and they showed
up without makeup and bodyguards the size of Volkswagen Beetles
with legs on them. They asked to come up and play and we did
stuff like 'Roll Over Beethoven,' maybe four or five songs. That was
back in 1977." It was a much smoother visit for Kiss than their first
visit three years before. There was the usual Kiss pyrotechnics at
the show, and Peter Criss's drum set was rigged to rise into the air.

Little problem: a low ceiling, no ventilation, and Criss was over-come by smoke and rushed to the hospital.

A few years later, a guy walked through the door who would settle in for a long stay—over a thousand shows. It was Decem-ber 1980, and Christie Smutak needed a promotion assistant. She was the marketing director for the Agora's Urban Cowboy brand, and put in a call to Cleveland State's WCSB-FM. Linas Johanso-nas picked up the phone. Nobody called him Linas. Johan was a lot easier to say. Smutak asked him to post the job opening, and Johan said, "I won't post it, but I'll be right over." He raced over to her office at Agency Recording, and two minutes later he became Smutak's marketing assistant. Was he in for a ride!

Talk about baptism under fire. Jonas (who died in May 2018), recalled, "There was actually a secret staircase from Agency Recording to the club. Buddy Maver was still the talent buyer, Suzy Peters was the marketing director, and I would help out down-stairs. January 1981, the first show of the year was the infamous Plasmatics show with Wendy O. Williams. We already knew she had gotten in trouble in Milwaukee the day before. Kathy Grund took care of the dressing rooms at the Agora, and had broken her leg. She came up to the Urban Cowboy marketing office and asked if she could hire me that evening to be her 'legs.' You know, carry a case of pop in, take that over there, put out the garbage. Whatever. Hell, yeah!" This was going to be some show.

"I remember that day vividly. It's backstage, it's the Agora, it's rock and roll! You're listening to the roadies and, of course, Wendy O. The tour manager was this big bald guy named Rod Swenson. Wendy came out dressed just in white panties, tennis shoes, and electrical tape over her nipples. It was against the law to expose nipples, but by the end of the show because she's sweating so much . . . holding a chain saw, smashing TVs . . . the electrical tape slipped off. Her panties are soaked with sweat and transparent. At that point, the bass player . . . this tall guy dressed in a ballet tutu with a Mohawk . . . is bouncing up and down. The ceiling at that part of the stage was low and it looks like he's hitting his head on a beam. There's blood running down his skull, but he keeps playing and doesn't miss a beat."

The show ends and the real fun begins. Johan looks over and, "There's Hank LoConti at the backstage entrance with Cleveland Vice Squad police, and they want to go back to arrest Wendy for indecent exposure. Well, according to the contract with the band there were no unauthorized personnel allowed in the dressing room. I just kept hearing Hank say, 'Do you have a warrant?' They didn't, so Hank said, 'Then you can't go back. Sorry.' All of a sudden Swenson walks out of the dressing room telling the stage manager, 'I need an ambulance!' We think it's for the bass player. Cleveland paramedics get there, they bring in a stretcher and close the dressing room door. The cops are still in the club arguing with Hank to get backstage. The door opens, here comes the gurney and they're wheeling out Wendy O! She wasn't hurt. It was their way of getting her out of the Agora. They couldn't arrest her until the next day at the Holiday Inn across from Cleveland State where the band was staying. That night I thought, 'Wow! This is frickin' rock and roll!' and I was hooked."

For Johan it was a case of right place, right time. "Kathy's leg was still mending for a while, and she asked if I wanted to continue doing that. Hell, yeah! By the time her leg healed a few months later she was so spoiled by me being her grunt guy that I stayed on working the dressing rooms with her." He recalls there were also a lot of groundbreaking acts coming through the club. "1981 was the year U2 played the Agora twice. By the time an act was at the Agora there was a reason they were there. U2 was almost like a religious experience. Kraftwerk played that year, and there were lots of acts in a very good year. The Go-Gos were there, and they wanted fish and Pepsi for dinner. Jane Wiedlin was acting like a little girl as she was playing with the fish she was eating."

If you wanted to know about the concert business, the Agora was the best classroom you could ask for.

"Hank taught me that when a band is on tour, it's like an assembly line of concerts," Johan recalls. "One night they're in Pittsburgh,

Cleveland the next, Detroit the following night. Hank's thing was that the show in Cleveland, the show they play for you, that's the show to see. You really want to make that night special for them and the audience. If you treat the band really well, you want them to come back and play for you again. Back then there was also this thing called 'promoter of record.' If you did the band first in the market, like 311 or Phish . . . well, the Agora did those bands first. They get bigger and want to come back, you get offered the act first for a set amount of money. If you say so, they can't go to another promoter. You can book bigger rooms because you're the promoter of record."

Johan says there were also name acts that played big houses yet still booked the Agora.

"December 1991 and we booked David Bowie with Tin Machine. The tour bus pulls up in the afternoon for sound check, and I was at the door to let them in. First person off the bus is David Bowie, and the first thing he says to me is, 'Will Jane Scott be at the concert tonight?' I told him she was onstage waiting for him, and Bowie said, 'Well, please take me to her!' There she was in the middle of the stage. What really impressed me about David Bowie was that he was the gentleman of rock. Considering what a big star he was, and the other people I had to deal with now and then, I was really surprised at how cultured and polite he was. He was so happy to see an old friend!

"The first thing Jane would do is pull out her old Instamatic camera, and she asked me to take a picture of them together. It wasn't until after her death [on July 4, 2011] that I actually got to see it. All that stuff ended up in the archives at the Rock and Roll Hall of Fame." That was a memorable show for another reason. "There was a couple whose first date was at the Tin Machine show. Front row in the mosh pit. When the guy wanted to propose he called me up to bring her down when there was no show going on. He brought her down blindfolded, and I met them at the stage door. He walked her down to the middle of the Agora stage and gave me a camera. Off comes the blindfold, and he said, 'Our first date was at this spot and I want to spend the rest of my life with you.'"

There was even a wedding on the Agora's stage—and what a wedding!

"Here's a story. There were two people that met at a Ratt concert at the Coliseum. Ratt was coming to the Agora Theater some years later and the couple came down to ask if they could get married at the Ratt concert. I gave them the number of Ratt's manager, and sure enough, Ratt was all over it. They got married between the opening act and Ratt during the intermission. It happened onstage and Ratt bought them a case of champagne and a wedding cake. We reserved the loges on the side, the opera boxes, for the family. The priest came out and we had the wedding march playing over the speakers. They did the ceremony in front of 2,000 people, and after 'You may kiss the bride'—hey, it was a heavy metal concert. You're not in a church and you're hearing stuff from the crowd. I'm thinking, 'The poor parents in the mosh pit having to hear that!' They had a ball that night! Ratt partied with them backstage and they brought their friends back there. You know that Stephen Pearcy is never going to forget that."

There even was a funeral at the Agora.

"Pappy Fagan died on a Saturday between two Meat Loaf shows on separate nights at Blossom Music Center. That was July 1994. Pappy was one of the Rowdy Roadies. He worked the backstage door, and if you wanted to get backstage at the Agora you had to get past Pappy. We went to his family and said, 'Look. Pappy would not want a funeral in a parlor or a church. That is not Pappy. We want to do the funeral at the Agora.' It was a memorial service, but it was also his funeral. That second night at Blossom, Meat Loaf mentioned Pappy's passing onstage and dedicated a song to him.

"A few weeks later we held the service at the Agora, and his funeral was a concert event. There was an ad in *Scene* and his name on the marquee. Instead of the memorial cards you see in funeral homes we had it on the ticket, 'Thanks for coming to Pappy's memorial service,' with the date. His funeral was an event and we held it in the ballroom. He'd been cremated and we had the urn there. Jack Daniels was being poured like crazy at the bar, and a group gathered outside the backstage door where you always saw Pappy and smoked a joint in his honor." Johan says they came this close to a baby being born at the club. "It was two hours short. It was an Inner Sanctum anniversary show, and one of the bands that was supposed to perform was called Rasch. It was named after Susan Rasch, the lead singer, and she was pregnant. She said, 'We're going to do the show. I'm going to be there', and a few hours before the show she started going into labor. After the show we got her to a hospital and the baby arrived."

Not all the memories were good, according to Johan.

"Not everybody was cooperative. A couple come to mind, and I'll chalk the first one up to being on the road. That's not an easy life. Where do you do your laundry? Who's taking care of stuff at home? Your bills? What about the family? When you work at a place like the Agora or CBGB's or the Roxy or whatever, you're getting to see one day in the life of. Whether it's Deborah Harry or Trent Reznor or whoever, it's only one day of their lives. We all have bad days. When Neil Young and the Blue Notes played the Agora—two or three songs from that show ended up on the Blue Notes' album—Neil Young wasn't exactly the nicest guy in the world that day. He was in a very bad mood, a lot of griping, but he was Neil Young. They were recording the show, and you just think he's having a bad day."

Sometimes artists made it bad for you.

"Ronnie Montrose really pissed me off. He was playing the ballroom, and even with 500 seats he couldn't sell it out. In his heyday he was never Eric Clapton. He's acting like he's still some arena star. The band that was touring with him was much younger, and Montrose wanted them in a separate room. He needed his own private room away from his band. Mind you, back then I was the guy who opened up in the morning, brought in the crews to load in, and I was the one who locked up at night. That was the only night I didn't lock up. 'Screw you, Ronnie. I'm not sticking around for this crap.' I went to Peabody's and I don't even remember who was playing there."

Some shows were scary.

"I had a show with Danzig and Soundgarden. I've noticed this with a lot of the Napoleon-like rock stars, meaning short in stature, like Ronnie James Dio. Glenn Danzig was one of them. Short, but he's built. During his show there was somebody in the mosh pit who was really agitating him. Giving him the finger. I don't know exactly what the kid was doing, but [Danzig] stops the song and he starts pointing to somebody in the mosh pit. It was like, 'You! I want you! I wanna kick your ass!', and I guess he pointed to the wrong kid. Danzig fans are very fanatical. They worship him like he's some sort of god, so when he pointed to this kid, who actually I don't think did anything, his fans picked the kid up and passed him up like body surfing to the stage like a sacrificial lamb. Literally threw him onto the stage, at which point Glenn starts beating up on the kid! In front of everybody!"

This was getting ugly real quick.

"I'm standing on the side of the stage at this moment and I'm watching Glenn beat up one of my customers. I tell whoever is standing around—stagehands, security—'Get Glenn off that kid and get the kid off the stage!' They separate the two and bring the kid to the side of the stage. My first comment to the kid was, 'Do you want to press charges?

"Noooo," he said. "I just want to know why he did this to me."

"Well, Soundgarden, Chris Cornell and his boys, come by and actually saved the day because all off a sudden they invited the kid onto their tour bus. Within 10 minutes this kid totally forgot what happened with Danzig. Screw Danzig. He's got new friends. He's partying with Soundgarden on the tour bus! Soundgarden saved Danzig from going to jail."

Johan says emotions could run high on and off the stage.

"Here's another story that ended up on MTV News. We had the Outfield at the Agora. During the middle of 'Josie', the hit, the lead singer throws off his guitar, smashes it, and walks off the stage. As he's walking off the stage he punches his tour manager in the face and proceeds to the dressing room. He slams the dressing room door and locks it, and all you start hearing is, *Smash! Crash! Boom! Bang!* You could tell he's throwing shit around the dressing room and we can't get in. He locked himself in. Finally, he lets his tour manager in and we end up finding out that a few days before that, there was like a hurricane-tornado situation in London and there was some damage. His wife and kids were still there in London while he was on tour. He kind of had a nervous breakdown in the middle of the show. We ended up getting a rebate on our guarantee. A lot of contracts will stipulate that the band has to play a minimum of 60 minutes. That was one of those concerts that lasted only 58 minutes. If he would have finished the song it would have been over 60. That was the end of the tour, and the crew had to hang out in Cleveland for like a whole week until a decision was made on what's going to happen. They ended up canceling the rest of the tour and the band flew back to England."

You can't tell the Agora story without mentioning Sue Csendes.

"It was early 1990 and I was working my full-time job at WHK, doing my college radio show, and was looking for more work as my day was finished at 1:30," she recalls. "I had quit my long-time job at the YMCA after a difference of opinion with the new executive director. I needed something to do to fill the day, so I asked Johan if he knew of anyone that I could 'deliver a package for.' What?! 'You know, deliver a package.' He still had zero idea what I was talking about. Although he probably did because when I went into a little more detail, his answer was 'You can't do that! Why are you even asking?' And I explained I needed something to do with my day. 'Show up Friday at 1:30 at the Agora, we're doing our first show there, you can answer the phones.'

"My favorite show for a really good vibe was the time Lenny Kravitz played the Agora. Every cross-section of people was at the show. White, black, old, young, rockers, alternative kids, hippies, everybody. A cool vibe and no problems."

Other shows left scars.

"On the other hand, we had three shows that were very, let's say, tense. A fraternity or sorority was having its national conference or get-together in Cleveland, and they rented the Agora for that evening's entertainment. They didn't have any national acts on the bill, maybe a DJ, but the capacity at the Agora was 2,100 if you included the balcony. At that time there were no sprinklers or fire systems in the club. We had to have a Cleveland fire person at every show monitoring the club."

The firefighters had a job to do and were quick to do it. Let's face it, no one wanted another incident like the 2003 fire in Rhode Island at which 100 people died.

"People were coming in and no one wanted to go upstairs," Sue continues, "so the Fire Department said we were at capacity for the main floor. We also had four Cleveland police working that night and had to tell people we were shutting the doors. It was like $20 a ticket. Two of the cops leave and we lock the doors." In retrospect, she says, they could have used the cops.

"The crowd starts pulling on the doors and breaks the locks. The promoter sees the evening going to hell in a handbasket really quickly, and our hands are tied because there's no place to put everyone if no one wants to go upstairs. Pretty soon it spills out onto the street, and the police have to shut down Euclid Avenue between East 40th and 55th! Okay, lesson learned. We have to avoid this type of situation in the future. Then they booked Bone Thugs-n-Harmony."

No group wants trouble at its shows. Trouble keeps people away from future shows, and acts don't need the grief or possible lawsuits. Sometimes a situation just gets out of hand, and in this case it stemmed from demand for space that wasn't available.

"As a rule, urban shows don't sell in advance," Sue says from experience. "There's usually a good-sized walk-up. Most of your sales are on the day of the show. I was in the box office, and they had some time before installed a thick pane of bulletproof glass. Plus, there was a heavy old wooden door. People are handing me cash, hand over fist, and the ticket was $20 or $40. I was running

Paul Simon filmed part of his 1979 movie *One Trick Pony* at the Agora, along with the B-52s and other acts. *(Janet Macoska)*

out of money in the cash drawer, so I started throwing the money into the box to move people through. I'm not sure what happened inside, but all of a sudden there were people running and screaming out. I don't know what's going on, but I said, 'Oh shit!' I scooped up the box of money to get away. Somebody smacked a big heavy metal stanchion against the box office window and then the door. We used to have a big metal sandwich board sign that was outside, and it was always getting blown over by the wind. As it turned out, someone brought the sign in and put it in my box office, and when the door got smashed open the sign fell and lodged itself against the door, blocking it. I was able to get away to the center office."

Then there was the Scarface show.

"It was a third-party promoter," according to Sue, "and this time we have metal bars on the box office door to reinforce it. Same thing, I'm sitting here with a box of cash. Again, and no one seems to know how or when it started, but things get out of control. They storm the bar and bottles of liquor are stolen, and then a security guard had to have surgery on his hand after he was thrown through a plate glass door. Bar stools were flying and a big couch we had was so bloodied up by injured people we had to get rid of it. Cops had left, and a security guard had to watch as a guy was getting beat up on the street because it was too dangerous to go out there."

She stresses such incidents were few and far between.

It didn't take a whole audience to disrupt a show either; one person can do that. Sue recalls a multimedia Pink Floyd tribute show that brought out the worst in a guy who decided to get naked except for one sock—before he jumped from the balcony. A woman who was nearby said she would never forget the sickening sound of the bones crunching in his face. In the ambulance you go, and next time stay off the chemicals.

Remember what Johan said about making the band comfortable so it will want to come back? That wasn't always easy, especially when it came to riders in the act's contract.

"We had Kenny G., the sax player, pull a tour together at the Agora. They rented out the theater, the lighting company shows up from Texas, the sound company shows up from Florida, and the band then shows up the next day. On the fourth day, I have to go pick up Kenny at Hopkins Airport. They rehearse for a couple of days, they put the light show together, pack up the trucks, and off on tour they go. Kenny only ate macrobiotic food. There was only one restaurant, on Noble Road, that made that kind of food. When we had David Lee Roth play the Agora we did the M & M's joke: the only M & M's he got were the brown ones. We did the Van Halen joke in reverse."

It wasn't just food.

"We would get things like a pack of tube socks or batteries. Double-A batteries. They would put a carton of cigarettes on there, and that's where you call the agent and say, 'Sorry, we're scratching off the carton of cigarettes.' Bands would always try to take advantage of the rider, whether it was to fill their tour bus with ice or beer or booze. If it's somebody big and important like David Bowie and he wants tube socks, I'm not arguing with the agent about it. They'll get what they want if they sell out the room."

For some, playing the Agora was like a homecoming.

"We had Chrissie Hynde, and it was the first and only time she played the building at East 55th," Johan recalls. "In the song 'Precious,' the first song of the first side of the first album, she sings about the building that the Agora was now in. Back when Johnny Dromette used to hold punk shows when it was the Hippodrome [not the theater that closed years before], she was a waitress at one of the diners on Prospect Avenue and she used to go there and watch shows. Then she would go down to the Euclid Tavern and hang out with Mr. Stress. When she played the Agora on the 'Independence Tour' she told the opening act to go to the next city—it was just going to be her band for the whole show. During the afternoon, Chrissie walks into my office and asks, 'You got a car?' Not a hello or anything like that. 'Yeah, but it's a Toyota Paseo. Why? You need a ride somewhere?' She said, 'No. I want to borrow it.' Here are the keys. Go ahead and smash it. She's got the money to buy me a new one. I ain't worried! She drove around the neighborhood—the Agora, Prospect, the Plaza Building where Pere Ubu lived back in the day. That evening when the show started, the stage was dark, the band starts playing and all of a sudden you hear her yell out, 'Hi Mom! I'm home!' Her parents were there, too. They came to any show that was related to them. They went to see Jim Kerr when Simple Minds played there because he's the dad of some of their grandkids.

"Before the show Chrissie came to me, actually during the day, and said, 'Here's the list of people I want backstage. By the way, here's the list of people I definitely don't want backstage.' It was all record company people. The only media people she wanted backstage after the show was Jane Scott. Everybody else on the list were like old girlfriends or roommates."

It's nice to get a thumbs-up, recognition that you did a good job. In March 2013, hundreds of people gathered at the Agora to "Thank Hank," as the event was called. There was a lot of confusion about the date and who would perform, but the big night did turn into a really special event in Cleveland music history. Lots of food and a river of booze, and the evening began with LoConti sitting on what appeared to be a throne while folks spoke about memorable moments with the man of the hour. Cindy Barber, Carlo Wolff, Buddy Maver, one after another, talked about his influence. As the "roast" segment came to a close, LoConti took the mic and told the crowd, "I thought this was supposed to be a roast. I didn't know it was going to turn into a love-in. I thought those went out in the '60s." Then came musicians representing a wide range of the styles that used to be featured at the Agora, including Foghat, Alan Greene, and Glass Harp.

A year later, Hank LoConti died at the age of 85. His career at one time covered as many as 12 Agoras, music festivals, overseas tours, a record label, a recording studio, and radio syndication. Records and CDs recorded live at the Agora from Todd Rundgren, the Cars, T. Rex, Bon Jovi, even Springsteen, pay tribute to a remarkable guy who created a legendary club.

Cleveland Municipal Stadium

1085 West Third Street, Cleveland

EVERYBODY JUST CALLED IT "the Stadium," the place where the Browns and Indians played, where Joe "Turkey" Jones pile-drived the Steelers' Terry Bradshaw, and Kenny Keltner ended Joe DiMaggio's record-breaking consecutive hitting streak. (It was also the site of a Billy Graham Crusade in 1994 just a short distance from where Howard Stern was holding one of his legendary "funerals" for his vanquished radio competitors.) Besides that, aside from an occasional truck pull or religious event, it sat empty most of the year. It was big, too: 80,000 seats in one of the largest non-college stadiums anywhere. The "Gray Lady by the Lake" just didn't get any dates!

It was rock and roll that gave Municipal Stadium a new lease on life, if only for a handful of memorable and very crowded events. When the Beatles became too big for conventional concert halls, their 1966 North American tour was forced to find places that could handle the expected demand for seats. WIXY 1260 had debuted on Cleveland's radio airwaves just a few months before, and station owners Norm Wain, Bob Weiss, and Joe Zingale had brought the Beatles to town in 1964 when they worked for WHK. Get Brian Epstein on the phone!

That call was made and a date was set. The Beatles would play Cleveland Municipal Stadium on August 14, 1966, the third date of the tour. WIXY would have its call letters on thousands of tickets that would sell themselves. At least that's the way it started out. The three got a bank loan, tickets were printed and were selling at a pretty fast clip, when all of a sudden . . . *thud!* A few weeks before the tour *Datebook* magazine ran segments of an interview

John Lennon did with Maureen Cleave in the *London Daily Standard*. He said Christianity would die out and the Beatles were more popular than Jesus.

Reaction was swift and ugly. Real ugly. Public burning of Beatle records and memorabilia. The Ku Klux Klan vowed to get the Beatles. Radio stations railed against the band, airplay for the new album *Revolver* ground to a halt—and three guys in Cleveland had tens of thousands of tickets to sell. Fifty years later, Norm Wain told *Boomer* magazine columnist Breanna Mona he was plenty worried.

"We had a lot of fun putting the show together. Then, two weeks before the show, the Cleveland Catholic Diocese hears that John Lennon said the Beatles are probably bigger than Christ and they said, 'No good Catholic would go to that show!'" Catholic or not, plenty of people started making other plans for that evening, and the day after, the bank would be expecting its money back for that loan!

They really didn't care whom they sold tickets to as long as they got money in return. Wain, Weiss, and Zingale jumped in their cars to drive to Toledo, Youngstown, Columbus, any city that wasn't hosting the Beatles. It wasn't easy. Wain flew to New York to meet Brian Epstein at a hotel. Wain laid it on the line about the guarantee, and Epstein said, "Come with me." They walked into another room, and there were the Beatles smoking cigarettes and playing cards. Epstein said, "Boys, this is Norm Wain from Cleveland." "Norm, hello! Cheers!" After a brief chat the guys said, sure, they would lower the number of guaranteed seats. That plane ride back to Cleveland was a little easier.

The Beatles still had a huge following, and tickets were still being sold, but at a relative trickle. Linda Gold remembers that show. In 1966 she was 15-year-old Linda Leibowitz and the concert for her was just a ride away on the Van Aken rapid line. She now admits, "I took the money from my mom," but Linda needed a ticket, and that was the fastest route to cash.

When all was said and done they sold about 25,000 seats.

Respectable, but come on—we're talking about the Beatles! The band arrived at the Sheraton Cleveland and met members of the press before the show. The big day arrived and Gold went down to the Stadium with a group of friends, but their seats were terrible. Plus, Gold was short and needed a better view of the stage. It was fine for the opening acts like the Cyrkle, but you really needed to see the headliners.

When the Beatles took the stage the Stadium erupted with screams, but about four songs in, things went south. It happened during "Day Tripper" when fans jumped out of their seats and rushed the stage. Linda saw an opportunity. "Everybody rushed toward the stage, and I'm like, 'So am I!' I may never see the Beatles again."

The crowd tore down a four-foot-high security fence, and a tsunami of people started heading toward the Beatles. Cleveland police weren't expecting this.

"Instead of watching the audience, they were watching the show," Wain recalled. "They had their backs turned to the audience, and they're looking at the show and enjoying it like everybody else. Meanwhile the audience was getting out of hand. It never occurred to them that maybe they ought to be facing the other way."

It was up to Wain and the WIXY jocks to restore order, and it wasn't pretty.

"Once they saw what we were doing, they started tackling people, too," Wain said. "By then they knew what to do. We taught them!"

The crowd was pushing ahead, and Gold was caught up in the mayhem. She managed to literally crawl out under some folks away from the crowd and found one of her friends. Who knew where everyone else was? They decided to wait out the rest of the show.

The Beatles were rushed off the stage until things calmed down.

According to *Boomer* magazine columnist Breanna Mona, the Beatles' road manager, Mal Evans, had to rush to stop wild packs of fans from grabbing instruments from the stage as mementos.

After a time, the band came out to finish, and another Beatles show went into the books. Any regrets? A major one, Wain says: He never got a photo with the band! Everyone thought they would be back the next year. A few weeks later they stopped touring for good.

About a week later, a small ad appeared in the *Plain Dealer* classifieds: "Beatle microphones used at Cleveland 1966 concert; 4 only. $200 each." Let the buyer beware.

That show put a cap on rock concerts at the Stadium for a while—until August 1973. Leon Russell had packed Blossom Music Center the year before for a show with Billy Preston, and the "Master of Space and Time" was on a career high. He was booked for a show at Municipal Stadium with soul singer Mary McCreary. They set up the stage about halfway down the field. It rained right up until the time Russell took the stage, but it was a good-sized crowd for a Wednesday night.

Now, who was going to put the meat in those 80,000 seats?

By 1974 Belkin Productions was considered among the most respected concert promoters in the country. WMMS was among a handful of the most powerful stations in the industry, and Northeast Ohio music fans had a worldwide reputation. Shows at Paul Brown Tiger Stadium in Massillon with Peter Frampton's Camel, Mott the Hoople, Uriah Heep, and other groups had come off with only minor problems, but the crowds had been only about 12,000. Cleveland Municipal Stadium was big enough to host a World Series. That wasn't about to happen soon the way the Cleveland Indians had been playing. But how about a World Series . . . of Rock!

They had a name; now they needed a lineup.

The bands for that historic first World Series of Rock show on June 23, 1974 were special guests Lynyrd Skynyrd and REO Speedwagon opening for Joe Walsh and Barnstorm and the Beach Boys. Tickets were pretty cheap, at $7 presale and $8 at the door for four bands, and Tokyo Shapiro audio equipment stores gave out discount vouchers.

Promoter Mike Belkin says people came to be part of the event as much as the music. "It grew because of what was going on there. Everyone was happy and enjoying the music. It was the place to be, and it just got bigger and bigger." He also says a well-oiled machine guaranteed everything ran efficiently. "We had everyone and everything when it came to putting on concerts. We were professional, had experience, whether it be the bands, the road managers, the stage hands . . . everything had been done before. I had someone call me that wanted to do a concert with Michael Stanley at an outdoor venue. We said they had to put down the proper covering so they don't kill the grass so they don't have to stop a ball game being played the next day. When you do enough concerts it comes naturally."

Okay, that came via trial and error. By the time the second show was staged a couple of weeks later, with Emerson, Lake & Palmer, the Climax Blues Band, and the James Gang, the turf was showing serious wear and tear. A month after that, when Crosby, Stills, Nash & Young headlined a show with the Band, Santana, and Jesse Colin Young, the grounds looked like a battlefield. That was on September 1, and the Tribe still had a month of games to go. Rumor was that 90,000-plus showed up for that show, way over legal capacity, but Belkin is quick to say that's not true. Still, it was a headache for the groundskeepers and something had to be done.

Let's take a closer look at that CSNY show. Crosby, Stills, Nash & Young were at their peak and did a long show with three sets, one acoustic and two electric. Some fans also took steps to enhance the experience.

You could smoke just about anywhere back then. Restaurants, college classrooms, theaters—if you had a place for ashes, you could smoke there. But most of the kids at the World Series of Rock weren't buying lids or ounces of Lucky Strike cigarettes. Legendary concert promoter Bill Graham, who was on the CSNY tour, saw cops bust a kid with some weed and was outraged. He raced up to Jules Belkin, shouting, "What the hell is going on here? I was just in the stands and a cop busted a kid for smoking a joint. I don't believe it! Do they arrest a football fan for taking a drink of booze

What a crowd! The Indians had a tough time drawing fans to the ballpark, but the "World Series of Rock" packed Municipal Stadium for a series of legendary summer concerts, including this first show, on June 23, 1974. *(Cleveland Public Library)*

at a game? It's a disgrace! Half the kids here are smoking. What are they going to do? Arrest them all? Your cops overreacted!"

They would have had to use Public Hall as a holding tank. With all deference to the former operator of the Fillmores East and West (and the Belkins and Graham had great respect for each other), the Belkins didn't control the cops and weren't about to tell them which laws to enforce. It was a practical matter, usually about how close the cop was. If he could smell it and you were close enough to grab, you would be getting a tap on the shoulder. A little discretion, and they turned a blind eye. Graham was also famous for overreacting. He fired the stage manager setting up the Cleveland show for building a stage eight-and-a-half-feet high instead of 19. "My performers get paranoid when they're that close to the audience," he claimed. Some felt that way when they were close to Graham.

Drug use was so prevalent at that show that the *Press* did a separate story on it, saying it was impossible not to get high and calling the atmosphere "euphoric." Joints were passed everywhere, along

Welcome home: Northeast Ohio favorite son Joe Walsh wowed the crowd at his 1974 World Series of Rock appearance with Barnstorm. *(Janet Macoska)*

with those silly looking wine skins. People openly rolled fatties with thick fingerfuls of ganja from plastic baggies. But some bad stuff circulated as well. There was enough concern about reports of bad THC that a warning was given from the stage. There were long pauses between acts so the stage could be set up as the show progressed, and people just lit up and "stayed cool, man."

Even Browns owner Art Modell was in awe of the turnout. He went on record praising concertgoers, saying he "saw rowdier fans at Browns-Steelers games." His concessions did good business, too. Mike Belkin had kind words for Modell: "Those were very positive concerts, and much of it was due to Art Modell being on the ball with what was going on. He let us do what we had to do."

So how many showed up for that show? Bruno Bornino at the *Cleveland Press* speculated 88,000. Jules Belkin said 82,648 but there were other estimates that as many as 90,000 showed up. Mike Belkin had lower numbers. Whatever the attendance, word got around that the show had set a record for the largest enclosed concert ever staged in the U.S., as well as the largest gross to that time. It drew from a wide area, with an estimated 30 percent coming from surrounding states and also including states as far away as South Dakota and New Mexico.

It was pretty hectic inside the Stadium. Cleveland's traffic commissioner, Henry Doberstyn, said about 20 kids were hospitalized for overdoses, and one either jumped or fell through a net near the home plate. He said despite the 141 off-duty cops and other security, it was pretty hard to stop people intent on hurting themselves. He was quoted saying, "If they want to commit suicide by using drugs, there's nothing much we can do." Three guys were spotted walking girders like a tightrope, unscrewing the big light bulbs with their shirts.

The next year, the Beach Boys were back, at the end of May 1975, co-headlining with Chicago. They didn't draw a rowdy crowd. It was the show two weeks later that drew attention, a four-act bill headlined by the Rolling Stones.

You couldn't bring bottles or cans into the Stadium, but fans would fill cheap wine sacks with liquor, and people sold weed, pills, and acid out in the open. The Cleveland Free Clinic had tents around the Stadium, and the shows kept them busy—with drunks jumping from the upper decks, overdoses, even sunburn.

There was another Stadium show that July with Yes, the Michael Stanley Band, and Joe Walsh. By the time the fourth show of the season rolled around, a five-band lineup headlined by Rod Stewart and the Faces, the grounds crew was tearing out its hair. There was heavy rain the next day and it ruined the field for the rest of the Indians season. The field had to be resurfaced, and they even had to replace a drainage system.

The 1976 World Series of Rock was canceled in a dispute over field seating—or standing, or whatever people did out there. A new covering was developed so the 1977 World Series concerts could be staged with shows from Ted Nugent, Pink Floyd, Peter Frampton, Bob Seger, and others.

The Pink Floyd show that June 25 was especially memorable. It was a full house at more than 83,000, sold out well before the gates opened for business. That didn't stop as many as 4,000 people who couldn't get tickets from showing up and heaving rocks and bottles at police and Stadium security. Three officers were injured and more than 70 people arrested, but they got off easy. Most of the arrests were for disorderly conduct and public intoxication, and fines were $25 each with $15 court costs.

Floyd's show started with the band's jet doing a low flyover that shook the Stadium rafters. A few minutes later the band tore into "Sheep" from their "Animals" LP and paper sheep on parachutes floated down on the fans. Some folks thought they were big rolling papers. Then the giant pig that can be seen on the album cover made its appearance. It was a Floyd love fest, so much so that the crowd screamed until it got a second encore. How much did it cost to put on that show along with the fireworks? In a nice way, Floyd's representative pretty much said, "None of your business." He told the *Cleveland Press*, "People don't want to know what things cost," and "Figures are for accountants."

The World Series of Rock became a rite of summer.

The shows sure kept maintenance crews busy all the way up West Third Street to Public Square. Even Modell had to admit that big crowds meant lots of litter. Streets were lined with paper, cups, smashed bottles, the occasional discarded pipe. Modell was also quick to say he was not responsible: "I can only control people in my ballpark. I am not responsible for what they do on the city streets." Modell said the Stadium was tidied up right away, except for a few broken windows.

The president of the Cleveland Indians, Ted Bonda, had a different opinion. When he entered the team's office there was an occasional broken window and a hole in the wall to boot. The Tribe had a game against the Orioles two days later, and fortunately the field was okay thanks to the plywood that had covered it during

Cleveland Press

Serving Its Readers for 100 Years

Saturday Final

No. 25725   Saturday, July 1, 1978

City becomes Rocktown as 86,000 fans roll in

By BRUNO BORNINO and SANDY BANKS

More than 86,000 music lovers insured with "a piece of the rock" — a $12.50 ticket to see Mick Jagger and the Rolling Stones — invaded downtown Cleveland today for the first Stadium, rock concert of the summer.

Thousands of young persons from across the country gathered outside the Stadium last night and early to-

day, some camping at the gates in hopes of getting ringside seats to gaze at the legendary Stones.

And although many of them were mere babes when the Rolling Stones first burst into prominence on the rock scene about 15 years ago, the Stones still rank high on their list.

"Rock is dead except for the Stones," proclaimed a Michigan State University student from Detroit.

The scene outside the Stadium resembled a street fair. The scent of marijuana wafted through the air, mixing with the music of the Rolling Stones that poured from speakers on top of cars and vans parked in the Stadium lot. Many radios were tuned to WMMS which was broadcasting Rolling Stones music.

The lot was filled last night by 11. Parking cost $5 which disgruntled some fans who pointed out that

parking normally costs $2.25 for Indians games.

One enterprising young man was selling beers for $1 a piece from his cooler to the Stadium crowd at 5:30 a.m. Another young man was doing a brisk business with a tattoo machine.

As the crowd grew larger, the party extended into downtown Cleveland, with concert-goers

Turn to Page A 2

The Rolling Stones opened the Stadium's 1978 concert season with a huge crowd, one of the biggest shows of their tour. *(Cleveland Press Collection, Cleveland State University Archives)*

the show. Cleveland's city street commissioner had crews working through the day.

The 1978 Series brought the Stones back on July 1, and two weeks later there was a show with just a hint of controversy. Electric Light Orchestra topped a bill with Foreigner and Journey, and ELO took the stage in a flying saucer. It later came out that some of the background music was prerecorded. Today that's a given but back then it bordered on scandal. It was also pretty tough to recreate the ELO sound onstage without a little help.

The Fleetwood Mac show that August had problems. People forget that performers are human and have the same problems we all do. That was the case with the Mac's Lindsey Buckingham, who ended up in a Washington, D.C. hospital with complications from a spinal tap the night the band was scheduled to play the Stadium. Jules Belkin got word of the last-minute cancellation while crews were setting up the stage. Canceling a show of this size puts a lot of people on hold. In this case, that meant 200 security guards, parking lot operators, food vendors, hotels, and—oh yeah—75,000

Crowds gathered well before the gates opened at Municipal Stadium for this 1978 concert so early arrivals could claim choice spots on the field. *(Cleveland Press Collection, Cleveland State University Archives)*

ticket holders. Fleetwood Mac took its fans very seriously, and the entire band, sans Buckingham, flew in by private plane for a press conference at the Bond Court Hotel to explain the situation and announce a new date, August 26. The group was accompanied by former member Bob Welch, now a solo artist and on that same Stadium bill with Eddie Money and the J. Geils Band. These were happier days for Welch and Fleetwood Mac; years later, after Welch filed suit against the band, it refused to have him join them at the Rock and Roll Hall of Fame induction. That August 26 date had been reserved for another World Series of Rock show starring Bob Seger, who stepped aside for Fleetwood Mac.

There were problems outside the Stadium. People leaving the show might be robbed while walking downtown after midnight. Many of the victims were from out of town and unaware of Cleveland's seamier street life. There were car breaks-ins, too. A Dayton woman found her car windows smashed and a collection of eight-track tapes gone. Oddly enough, a .357 magnum she brought along for protection was also missing. Cleveland Police grabbed a guy who was firing shots outside the Stadium, but they had to chase him all the way to Public Square before they got him. Another woman found her car jacked up in the Stadium parking lot with two wheels missing. There were also plenty of street corner evangelists spreading the anti-rock and roll word to concertgoers as they exited the Stadium. "You need religion!" one zealot said to one. The kid pointed back at the Stadium and said, "I just got it! In there." Despite the problems, Cleveland police called it the best-behaved of the summer's Stadium shows to date, with the least number of incidents connected to violence, drugs, or illegal fireworks.

Fleetwood Mac was probably the biggest name in music at the time, and the World Series of Rock shows were sponsored by WMMS. So, what do you do if you're a competing radio station when a huge band comes to town and you don't have a piece of it? That was the position that WWWM—or M105—was in. They were able to buy tickets for giveaways, and the band helped out with an autographed catalog of their albums for a contest prize. Other than that you have little choice other than to welcome the band and pretend the show isn't sponsored by your competitor.

When Buckingham returned the band walked onto the Stadium stage to a huge flurry of fireworks. Ultimately, the show ran over eight hours. The changed date had caused some lineup juggling so Todd Rundgren could catch a flight to Chicago for a couple of shows and so both Eddie Money and Welch could get to and from St. Louis. It was a homecoming of sorts for one musician: Ben Orr of the Cars, who was known as Ben Elevenletters when he was in Cleveland playing with the Grasshoppers. (There were eleven letters in his last name, Orzechowski.)

It would be naïve to think that a stadium full of people could come back month after month, year after year, without incident. Only one Stadium show was scheduled for 1979, and it seemed to have a bad vibe. It was a pretty hard-rocking lineup: Scorpions, AC/DC, Thin Lizzy, Journey, Ted Nugent, and Aerosmith. None of the bands was known for acoustic music. Fans would often travel long distances and wait outside the Stadium overnight to be first in for good spots. More than a dozen reported being robbed, sometimes by gangs of up to 50 people. Police made arrests for drunkenness, drugs, disorderly conduct, and robbery; 35 knives were confiscated at the show, and there were so many fireworks in the crowd that the performers said they were concerned for their own safety. There were reports on the day of the show that dozens of people were stumbling around, glassy-eyed and vomiting. Some passed out, and staffers from the Free Clinic rushed over with stretchers while fans just walked around them. There were fistfights, and one guy was almost thrown off a pedestrian bridge. When the concert let out, there were reports of hundreds, maybe thousands of fans harassing small groups of cops and targeting their cars before they pulled out. As many as 37 people were treated at St. Vincent Charity Hospital, some because of fights between black people and white people. The worst was a huge fight at the Stadium's Gate D that ended up with five shootings, including one fatality.

The concert got rave reviews. The front page headlines told a different story.

By Monday, newspapers were asking who was responsible for the safety of concert goers. Even though it was during Cleveland city council's summer recess, councilmen Ceasar Moss and James Carney called a meeting of the safety committee. They planned to question promoters and police about the events surrounding the show and made it clear if nothing could be done to ensure the safety of fans, "then we'll have to stop the concerts." Jules Belkin assured police and politicians he was "terribly appalled and very concerned" by the events, but still had every intention of staging the next World Series of Rock show in less than three weeks. Moss suggested the violence was a direct result of drugs and booze linked to the show, but Belkin countered, saying, "We've had over one million people attend concerts at the Stadium in the last four years without any killings or major violence." He didn't see a link to the concerts and said, "This kind of thing affects all kind of events at the Stadium.

Fans fly the flag from the Stadium stands for a World Series of Rock concert in 1980. *(Cleveland Press Collection, Cleveland State University Archives)*

"The last time someone got killed in the city, did we close down the city?" Belkin said, knuckling down. "We're proud of what has happened music-wise in Cleveland, and we have no intention of taking our concerts anyplace else. Those concerts planned downtown will stay downtown." There was plenty of security on hand for the show. There were 225 off-duty cops and security forces outside the Stadium before and during the concert, but anything can happen with a crowd.

What was it like backstage? Lots of egos and a potential for disaster. Even so, Belkin says, "They were all positive. Our security was really good so we never had any problems backstage. We didn't have people at that point being able to rush the stage because it was too high. There weren't any events that were really memorable as to what was happening backstage."

One incident may have changed the future of a major band.

Hot time in the summer: Concertgoers, both male and female, were seen in various stages of undress as the heat beat down on Municipal Stadium. You saw plenty of plastic bags, too, often with stuff that wasn't legal.
(Cleveland Press Collection, Cleveland State University Archives)

Aerosmith's Joe Perry tells the story in his book *Rocks*. There was already a lot of tension within the band. Then, after Aerosmith played its Stadium gig, band members learned of a dressing room fight that had started when Elyssa Perry threw a glass at bassist Tom Hamilton's wife, Terry. It may have been the spark that drove Perry from the band for several years.

Even Cleveland mayor Dennis Kucinich got involved. To forestall another series of violent incidents, Kucinich asked that the Stadium show be rescheduled a day earlier, from Sunday August 18. The upcoming concert was to feature Foreigner, Kansas, the Cars, the Tubes, and David Johansen. That concert was not to be. Despite earlier praise for the crowds, Stadium Corporation head Modell pulled the plug on further shows, at least for the rest of that year.

There also was serious concern about safety. The public kept the controversy going as well. A nurse wrote to the *Plain Dealer* describing a gunshot victim's fight for life after the show. She went on about stabbings and overdoses, and a headline called the event a "deathtrap." Word of mouth is a powerful weapon.

Speaking for the Belkins, Jim Marchyshyn said the promoters and even sponsor WMMS were getting a lot of calls from concerned parents. After a meeting with Kucinich, Mike Belkin, and Police Chief Jeffrey Fox, the Foreigner/Kansas Stadium show was canceled. The show would have run late, with little public transportation, and it made sense not to worry parents. Kucinich's press secretary was quoted as saying, "Mr. Belkin's business is to promote concerts, and ours is to promote public safety. If he decides to cancel a concert, it's his business."

Most of these concerts were rescheduled. People wanted to see these hot acts, so the promoters moved a couple of dates to the Richfield Coliseum. Only Foreigner had to cancel, with the Cars and former New York Doll David Johansen on August 18, and with Kansas with the Tubes the next evening. Still, there was a rumbling in Richfield Township as trustees attempted to stop the shows. To halt them, they would have had to establish that the crowds "would result in danger and harm to the community, either by interfering with property rights, by being a danger to public health and safety or injuring the public." Fat chance. There had been concerts at the Coliseum for years, and at least one trustee admitted he and his fellow trustees didn't have the authority to determine what acts would be booked at a private facility.

The last official World Series of Rock show was held at the Stadium on July 19, 1980. It featured the J. Geils Band, Eddie Money, Def Leppard, and Bob Seger with the Silver Bullet Band—and lots of changes in crowd control. There were 12,000 reserved seats, metal railings to guide you through ticket takers, and no waiting overnight for gates to open. The parking lots opened at 6 a.m., and you weren't allowed near the ball yard until two hours later. The Free Clinic had a small army of volunteers and staff on hand with a main tent and five smaller tents, five doctors, 18 nurses and dozens of other staff. Again, only a small percentage of the tens of thousands needed emergency care, about one-half of 1 percent of those attending, but that still meant hundreds. The Cleveland Police Narcotics unit also warned of pushers with a built-in clientele and said phony pills were common. There was also the animal tranquilizer PCP, heroin, and LSD, so let the buyer beware; wash it down with booze, wine, or beer, and you would be dancing with the devil. Add to that the possibility of phony tickets for sale outside the Stadium, maybe even grabbed from your hand as you stood in line. Jane Scott of the *Plain Dealer* advised women to carry purses that shut tight or, better yet, just pin cash inside a pocket with your ID. Scott always pinned her ticket to her lapel when she entered a show.

The show came off pretty much without a hitch. A fistfight here or there and a few dozen overdoses, but it was the heat, a high of 93 degrees, that caused the most problems for the Free Clinic staff. By all accounts the show was smaller, about 50,000, but successful. Even so, it was time to fold the tent on the World Series of Rock.

There would be plenty of other shows at Municipal Stadium, including one by U2 one rainy night as Bono performed with his arm in a sling. There were shows by the Who, Bruce Springsteen, Pink Floyd, and Michael Jackson and the Jacksons Victory Tour. The Rock and Roll Hall of Fame held a massive grand opening celebration concert there with Len "Boom" Goldberg from WMMS doing stage announcements. It seemed like déjà vu from the World Series of Rock.

How tough was it to put on those shows?

"I don't know that it was a nightmare," Mike Belkin says, looking back. "We knew what to expect, and that was based upon experience. That wasn't the first time the bands had played Cleveland. There was never a situation with, 'Oh my god this is a lousy audience!' We had a good reputation when it came to concerts. Those were concerts plus!

"I don't know if we had lessons learned," Belkin adds. "We found

it easier to do and not as many headaches that might have happened when we first did them. You had problems with the Indians
and the grass at the Stadium turning light. We had to put down
special plywood and we had to change that to a covering. That
was the most important thing as far as planning the dates at the
Stadium. Modell was so cooperative. He was the key."

Was there an act the Belkins couldn't get? There was, but it had
nothing to do with the World Series of Rock. "I put in an offer for
the Beatles," Belkin says. "I don't remember which one didn't want
to do it. I tried a couple of times and gave them some stupid offer."
Later reports put that figure at $4 million! Most stadium-wor-
thy acts other than the Beatles did play the World Series of Rock,
however, and Paul McCartney sold out the Stadium in 1990. In
1996, Cleveland said goodbye to Municipal Stadium. It was demol-
ished to make way for the new Cleveland Browns Stadium on the
same site, just down the street from the Rock and Roll Hall of
Fame.

Smiling Dog Saloon

3447 West 25th Street, Cleveland

FOR A LONG TIME, it was said that all the culture in Cleveland was on the east side of the Cuyahoga River. Museums, the orchestra, theaters, and nightclubs from downtown and near East 105th fell under that umbrella. But pockets on the west side bucked that trend, as the Smiling Dog Saloon at West 25th Street and Woodbridge Avenue illustrated.

The club at 3447 West 25th opened in October 1971 after antiques dealer Roger Bohn and his partner Ben Bilynsky decided to try the club scene. They took over the old Marvin Recreation building, which had a pool hall and bowling alley, moved in tables and a stage and started booking acts. They decorated the bar with different pieces of art all depicting smiling dogs. Why smiling dogs and why name a bar after one? As Bohn once said, it all started with the van he used to transport antiques. He said, "One day someone put a sticker on the truck that said, 'Never trust a smiling dog!'" The name stuck.

Cleveland had a strong jazz scene at the time and it was relatively easy to book top-name national acts in the club for the right price. Herbie Hancock, Sun Ra and his Arkestra, Mose Allison, and blues great Freddie King headlined early on, and there were plenty of rock and folk acts, too.

Ellen McIlwaine stopped by the WMMS studios for a live performance to plug her gig at the Smiling Dog and became the first recording artist in the station's long running Coffee Break Concert series. Alex Bevan was a favorite, and Gram Parsons and Roger McGuinn, former members of the Byrds, played gigs there a few months apart. The club booked comedy with Firesign Theater's Phil Proctor and Peter Bergman, progressive rock with Annie Haslam and Renaissance, the all-female rock group Fanny, and early glam punk with New York Dolls. The club also booked the first appearance of Lynyrd Skynyrd north of the Mason-Dixon line (not long after, the band was signed to co-headline the massive World Series of Rock at Municipal Stadium).

The concerts were aired late Saturday night on WMMS, and they exposed a lot of different musical genres to what was basically an FM rock audience.

By early November 1973, just about two years after its opening, the Smiling Dog was named the top vote-getter in the *Plain Dealer's* Favorite Tavern contest. It was more for bragging rights, but the Dog beat out Pat Joyce's, Kiefer's, and the Leather Bottle, all of which had been around a lot longer. In the days before microbreweries Cleveland still had a large local brewery, C. Schmidt & Sons, that bottled Schmidt's and Duke beer. It kicked in for a first-place trophy and $500 to the *Plain Dealer* Charities in the Smiling Dog's name.

The Dog was getting pretty aggressive in booking major names for the club and bigger venues. Weather Report and Brian Auger had gigs lined up at Case Western Reserve University, and Billy Preston, who helped fill Blossom Music Center with Leon Russell the year before, was scheduled for the Allen Theatre but had to cancel. They weren't big enough to take on the Belkins, but they weren't restricted to the four walls of the club. In addition, Odetta, a mainstay at La Cave, found a new home at the Dog when La Cave closed. Odetta exemplified how foreigners appreciate our culture more than we do. She played to standing-room-only audiences in Japan and much of Europe, but small clubs when she was in the states.

The Dog kept booking acts and making much of its money at the bar, but there was one gig where the bar was not an option. Glenn Schwartz had reached mythical status as the original guitarist for the James Gang and later Pacific Gas & Electric. Then

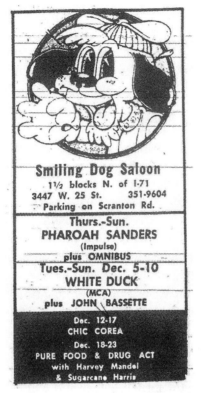

The Smiling Dog Saloon hosted some of the biggest names in contemporary folk and jazz and even members of the Firesign Theater comedy troupe.

he became deeply religious and formed the All-Saved Freak Band. When he did a benefit for the Kent New Generation Church, that also meant no liquor sales.

Booze was not the issue a few months later when the Edwin Hawkins Singers brought in what was described as the "sound of a spirited storefront church" to the Smiling Dog. Granted, it had been a few years since they hit with "Oh Happy Day," adapted from an old church hymn with new lyrics and a revised melody, but Hawkins still brought a show heavy on gospel. He also mixed in some Stevie Wonder and even Barbra Streisand's "The Way We

Were," but stressed that his gospel roots were "a ministry within itself."

By 1975 there was serious competition on the local club scene. Patrons can be fickle, and the Agora was pulling in big names and broadcasting a lot of those shows in prime radio time during the week on WMMS—effectively one-hour commercials. Jazz had a smaller and loyal audience, but you need revenue flow to keep a club alive. Although the Smiling Dog closed in 1975, some were optimistic it could be revived. A letter in the *Plain Dealer* in late 1976 asked about rumors the Dog would reopen in the old WHK Auditorium at 5000 Euclid. The bad news was that Roger Bohn had ended talks with the building management, and the Dog would remain a memory. By the way, that letter was written by Jim Henke, a local musician and writer who would become one of the key people at the Rock and Roll Hall of Fame.

The building on West 25th would continue as a music club under different names including the Deputy Dog, which ventured into hard rock with bands like Fury and a black heavy metal band called Black Death. It later became known as the Magic Show Palace, featuring acoustic acts, and in 2002 it was bought by Jim Mileti, the son of the former owner of the Coliseum at Richfield. He renamed it the Winchester Music Hall and brought in major acts, including Chad & Jeremy, Molly Hatchet, and a long line of others. But Mileti stunned the club's fans in 2014 when he pulled the plug on the Winchester. A born-again Christian, he told the *Plain Dealer* that "plying people with booze is not making friends with God. It's more important to do what's right and walk upright with the Lord."

With that, another legendary venue finally faded into history.

Musicarnival

4401 Warrensville Center Road, Warrensville Heights

As we've said, great rock and roll can be seen anywhere, from basements to ballrooms, cow fields to coliseums. Even a tent. Musicarnival was basically a circus tent on a street corner and was billed as "theater in the round." That meant summer tours with acts like Robert Goulet and Phyllis Diller and stage productions like "South Pacific" and "Guys and Dolls." Musicarnival opened in June 1954 and really wasn't in business that long—a little over 19 years. In that time, it presented some of the most memorable shows in rock's still-brief history.

You couldn't miss the place, right next to Thistledown Race Track at Warrensville Center Road and Ellacott Parkway. Warrensville Heights City Hall and the police department were just across the street, as was the municipal swimming pool. When rock bands started getting booked at Musicarnival you could hear the midday sound checks from poolside, and if you liked what you heard you could wander over for an autograph.

Living nearby were Warrensville High grad Steve Nemeth, better known on WZAK and WMMS as "Doc Nemo," and Tom Rezny, a Bedford High graduate who would take the air name "T.R." on WWWM (M105) and WMMS. Both were pioneers in early FM progressive rock radio.

Musicarnival was pretty innovative for its time. People sat in canvas chairs and watched musicals and plays during a summer season, and they didn't have to go downtown to catch shows. Still, it takes time to cast and rehearse a show, and eventually Musicarnival founder John L. Price Jr. started booking stage acts to keep the tent busy. Empty seats on off nights means no revenue flow, so he decided to make the tent available for rock bands. Years before, the owners had expanded to 2,300 seats. It was cheaper to book Musicarnival than a theater—or Cleveland Music Hall, which could hold the same number. By 1967, Musicarnival management started thinking about booking rock acts.

Roger Abramson had left Belkin Productions to start his own production company, A Friend Productions. "I was born in Painesville but moved to Cincinnati when I was very young," Abramson says. "I was doing very well there as chairman of one of the major civil rights organizations, and I was inducted into the Civil Rights Hall of Fame. Plus, there was the Ohio Valley Jazz Festival. In 1968, Mike Belkin got these dates for Aretha Franklin . . . I think it was Louisville, Cincinnati, Columbus . . . and he needed someone to promote in these cities. I did the shows for him, and afterwards he came up to me and was very happy. 'Why don't you come to Cleveland?' I went to Cleveland with a bonus and a new Cadillac and moved to Shaker Heights." Belkin Productions was also a very young company at the time.

"When I first got there I was working off a shelf in the back of [Belkin's] clothing store at West 25th and Clark. Then we moved to an office across the street." Abramson also saw the company grow quickly, along with the rising local music scene. "I was only in Cleveland for a short time, about three years. In that time Belkin Productions became one of the biggest production companies in the Midwest. They asked me to join them when we met in Cincinnati, and I was able to sign the James Gang."

Here's how that went.

"I went out to Kent State," he recalls. "[Drummer] Jimmy Fox wanted to be with Belkin, but at first they weren't interested. I went out and talked to them and signed them, and they had already had a contract with ABC Records and Bill Szymczyk, who produced them. At the same time, I also signed Michael Gee [Michael Stanley] who had a group called Silk, who Szymczyk also did at ABC." Abramson would himself go on to manage Tiny Alice, Eli Radish, and the Pure Prairie League.

Musicarnival's theater-in-the-round concept drew long lines for its summer series
of shows. Rock bands drew crowds, too—but they were dressed a lot more casually.
(Cleveland Public Library)

It was a simpler time for the concert business.

"The record companies didn't dictate terms for artists—who's
on the bill with whom," Abramson says. "You could put together
Frank Zappa and the Mothers of Invention with the MC5 out of
Detroit, and New York street singer David Peel and the Lower East
Side. You could have three acts from three different labels. But that
was before the corporate takeover of rock and roll."

There was quite a learning curve for both artist and promoter
in those early days.

"I put the James Gang on the show opening for the Who at
Cleveland Music Hall. James Taylor was on that bill, too, and I
don't know if he didn't want to play before the James Gang, but he
was the bigger act. Afterwards, Pete Townshend told *Rolling Stone*
that Joe Walsh was the best guitarist in America. I told the agent
that James Taylor should open up the show because he wasn't
going to be able to follow the James Gang."

Abramson was right. Taylor pretty much got booed off stage,

and made it a point to never appear in that kind of set-up again
without a backing band. On the other hand, the Who and James
Gang got along famously and even went on tour together.

Abramson notes American humor was sometimes lost on the
Who: "I remember the James Gang were opening for the Who on
some dates, and at one show during the Who's set, Walsh mooned
Pete Townshend. Pete got really mad."

At first, musical acts at Musicarnival were pretty tame: Sam the
Sham and The Pharaohs, Keith, the Royal Guardsmen, Simon &
Garfunkel, Tommy James and the Shondells. Nothing out of the
ordinary and no problems. When the Lovin' Spoonful played the
tent, fans sat and applauded politely. One even asked another to
keep it down so everyone could hear the music. Maybe some of the
edgier acts could get booked, too. There was this new group out of
Los Angeles called the Doors. Let the experiment begin.

"We [Belkin Productions] did all the Doors shows east of the
Mississippi. Bill Graham [of Fillmore fame] had them west of the
Mississippi," Abramson says. "We had a hard time, hoping that Jim
[Morrison] would even show up. We had a rather large person who
was his security guy who stayed with him. We tried to make certain
he would be at the shows. He was like the James Dean of music,
so rebellious. You feel bad when you hear about these great, great
people who keep losing their lives because they don't take care of
themselves."

This was the Doors' first tour of the Midwest so they had a lot
riding on it. When the night of September 14 rolled around, the
band took the stage and Morrison wandered over to the mic. He
was dressed in black leather, and his eyes were at half-mast. He
played around with a red light, looked around the stage and then
let out a huge belch. This wasn't a "whoops! Excuse me" burp. This
was a gut-wrenching, keg-party boom like a lion's roar, so the folks
in the last row knew what you had for lunch. Problem was, no one
was in the back rows. Only 700 people showed up, so everyone had
a pretty good seat. Morrison wiped his mouth and said, "This is
one of the finest tents I've ever belonged to, but where is everybody,

man?" Didn't matter. The band tore into "Soul Kitchen," "Back Door Man" and the rest of their first album in what may have been Morrison's best performance in Cleveland. Just to keep people on their toes, at one point he screamed "Wake up!" at the audience and they yelled right back at him. When the show ended Morrison stumbled back to the dressing room, and as he got to the door he fell to his hands and knees and crawled in.

Soon after Abramson started A Friend Productions (with shows brought by "A Friend"). Local artist Jay Vecchio did Fillmore-quality designs for posters and print ads. He later turned up as a member of Deadly Earnest and his Honky-Tonk Heroes. A Friend also turned into a load of work for Roger Abramson.

"I was very serious about what I did, and it was hard," Abramson says. "I had to come up with all the deposit money. There was no corporate sponsorship. I did have a group of Clevelanders who were investors, but it was very important to do everything correctly." Abramson also says there was rich potential for growth. "A Friend worked in five cities. They brought out a lot of folks with a feeling of warmth and charisma. Everything is so advanced now, not like the hand-to-mouth thing that we used to do."

Many of these acts, too, were just starting out, so it was a great opportunity to see superstars in the making. That brings us to the Who. It was July 14, 1968, sunny and warm. A great night for a show, and what a show it turned out to be. The opening band was Cyrus Erie, local favorites as close to an American version of Mods as you were likely to get. Cyrus Erie featured Eric Carmen and Wally Bryson, who would go on to be lead singer and lead guitarist in the Raspberries.

The Who was having equipment issues, so Cyrus Erie let them use their amps. The show turned out to be classic Who, with Pete Townshend doing windmills on his guitar, Roger Daltrey swinging his mic in wide circles, Keith Moon drumming like a machine gun and John Entwistle playing bass lines you could feel in your stomach. The promoters asked for four off-duty cops for security, but only one showed up. At this point Bryson might have been

No corner seats: The round stage worked for lounge type acts and comedy,
but setups for rock bands usually meant more than a few obstructed views.
(Cleveland Public Library)

rethinking that equipment loan. Townshend shoved his guitar into
one amp, threw another on the floor—and then the crowd came
up to join them on stage. Taking pictures, sticking paper flowers
on stuff, taking Moon's drumsticks, and the Who seemed to be
having a great time. Instruments got smashed and lots of people
went home with souvenirs. The cop on duty may have gone home
with less hair.

The Musicarnival audience didn't put up with delays. Vanilla
Fudge found that out the hard way that August. To be fair it may
not have been the band's fault. They showed up at the airport
thinking they were flying first-class from Chicago. Surprise! They
were booked on standby, and finally got a flight through Lafayette,
Indiana. The Damnation of Adam Blessing kept the crowd enter-
tained as long as they could, but when the Fudge walked on stage

three hours late the crowd greeted them with boos. Airports and rock bands weren't always a good mix. Some crew members for the band Cactus got popped at Hopkins Airport in August 1971 when a stewardess on a Northwest Orient flight out of Chicago thought they were smoking weed. Oddly enough, two members of Cactus, Tim Bogert and Carmine Appice, were also in Vanilla Fudge. The cops said they were clean and didn't detain them. The incident later turned up in a song titled "Mean Night in Cleveland."

Like the August 1978 Springsteen date at the Agora, certain shows are so legendary people tend to forget they were not there. If everybody who claims to have seen Led Zeppelin July 20, 1969 at Musicarnival actually had, that show would have had to be held at Max Yasgur's farm. It was a big show, but within the limits of the tent.

Zeppelin's debut album had been out for about six months, and a new one was due before the end of the year. Early FM rock radio loved the LP, and that was the target audience. The Musicarnival date sold out quickly, but an unforeseen issue hung over the tent: The concert was the same night as the Apollo 11 landing. In theory, it wouldn't be a problem because the astronauts were due to step on the moon after midnight.

The concert got off to a roaring start with the James Gang. Joe Walsh had replaced lead guitarist Glenn Schwartz the year before, and the band was developing a huge reputation all around the Midwest. A bit of rock history may have been planted that night, courtesy of Walsh. In 2008, his daughter Lucy was asked in an interview if her dad filled her with stories about Cleveland. She laughed and said, "My dad has never told me a story the same way twice!" But she added, "One day Jimmy Page called our house and my dad wasn't home. Jimmy told me my dad gave him the guitar he used for the solo on 'Stairway to Heaven.'" When was that? Walsh did play as a solo act on a bill with Led Zeppelin in 1975, but that was after "Stairway" had been released. Was that exchange made in Warrensville Heights?

It was finally time for the headliner, and Zeppelin hit the stage

Every day was an adventure at Musicarnival, which opened its
tent flaps to promoters from across the city. You could have
acts like Phyllis Diller performing on stage just hours after
Jim Morrison and the Doors. *(Cleveland Public Library)*

with fury. Bless *Plain Dealer* rock critic Jane Scott. Everyone loved
her, fans and musicians alike, but it was obvious that she was a
lot older than the acts she covered. She compared Robert Plant
to a male Janis Joplin (which admittedly was in the ballpark), but
she said his "collarbone-length hair looks like a cheap permanent
caught in the rain." She was impressed by his "$60 python boots"
and wrote that Plant "murmurs words and syllables like Cab Calloway." Well, hi-de-hi-de-ho!

Abramson was wrapped up in details of the show behind the
scenes. Looking back, he said Zeppelin was not going to be a sure
bet: "At the time, Led Zeppelin had not had a No. 1 record. It was
their first album. I do remember the impact Robert Plant had on
the young women there."

To Jane Scott's credit, she did a credible job describing the band's
musicianship and individual talents. After a 10-minute "Dazed and
Confused," the band left the stage to screams from the audience
for more. That was when they got word that the first moon walk
had been moved up. They all wanted to see it. Zeppelin came back
on stage and said they would do just one more tune so everyone

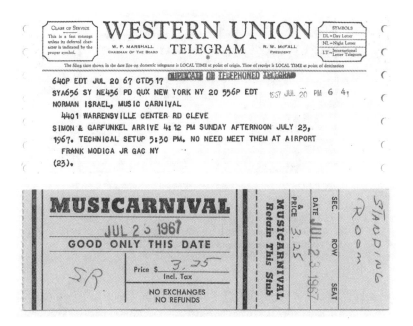

Going my way? Simon and Garfunkel made it easy on promoters when they re-scheduled their Musicarnival appearance. The show was so hotly anticipated that Musicarnival actually issued standing room only tickets to keep up with demand. *(Cleveland Public Library)*

could witness history. After a killer version of "Communication Breakdown," the band jumped into limos and raced down to the Somerset Inn on Warrensville Center near Van Aken Boulevard. Together with members of the James Gang, Scott, and the *Cleveland Press*'s Bruno Bornino, they watched Neil Armstrong take "one giant leap for mankind." Years later during a satellite radio interview, Plant was asked about Apollo 11 and he said one word: "Cleveland."

A lot of bands played the tent in those years, ranging from folk with Arlo Guthrie and Kate Taylor, country-tinged rock with the Flying Burrito Brothers, British boogie-woogie with Long John Baldry, and a sort of inspired farce with the Mothers of Invention. But a pair of shows in summer 1971 gave Northeast Ohio its last

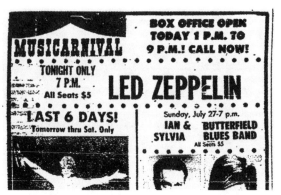

One small step: Led Zeppelin's Cleveland debut at Musicarnival was a prelude for a watch party at a nearby Shaker
Heights motel for the Apollo XI Moon landing. Members of
the band remembered it years later. *(Cleveland Public Library)*

look at a virtuoso guitarist. It was a Sunday night in August, and
the Allman Brothers were on the verge of superstardom. They had
released two critically acclaimed studio albums, and a double live
LP had just been issued the month before. Duane Allman also
played second lead guitar with Eric Clapton on Derek and the
Dominoes' *Layla and Other Assorted Love Songs*, and the Allman
Brothers Band had been hand-picked by Bill Graham to close his
Fillmore East the previous June. Abramson says the band had an
impact on his life in a different way.

"I loved the Allman Brothers. We started a relationship there
at Musicarnival and it went on from there. We had a particular
relationship because I have kind of an adopted son, Gregory, and
he ended up being one of the roadies and was with them for quite
a while. His mother was in jail and he lived with a preacher in
Shaker Heights. Because we lived there he met my children, who
were about his age, and before you know it he was hanging out
all the time at our house." Gregory was a big guy, too, over 6 feet
tall, so he put him to work at Musicarnival. "He was just the best
worker I've ever seen. He was security, he was running around the
tent. He looked at my wife and me as his mother and father." Even

after he left the Allmans, Gregory still called home to "mom and dad" on a regular basis.

There were two Allman Brothers shows, both sold out, but at the last minute the band had to move them back to 6 and 9:30 p.m. It was common for fans without tickets to hang around the parking lot and then rush under the tent, which is what happened at the second show. A packed house, and then, after the show, a surprise as cars left the lot: Duane Allman stood at the gate and thanked people in each car as they pulled out onto the street. He would die in a motorcycle accident that October.

A Friend Productions also promoted the earliest Northeast Ohio shows by one of the most important bands of the progressive rock era. Abramson notes, "We did Pink Floyd at the Akron Civic Theatre and at Emerson Gym at Case Western Reserve. It's when they were just introducing quadraphonic sound. At Emerson Gym they had speakers all over, and when they had the sound of footsteps it sounded like they were walking across the top of the gym ceiling!" In 1972, Abramson also had a hand in staging the huge "A Day to Remember" free benefit concert, which drew massive crowds. He recalls, "One time I did a benefit for the Cleveland Free Clinic at Edgewater Park. There were more people than you could ever imagine at an outdoor show. The show was supposed to end at 10:30, and we still had the headliner, Fanny, to go on. I got to Mayor Ralph Perk, and he said he would come down and see what was going on. He came down with Dennis Kucinich, and Kucinich got on stage and said, 'Let the show continue.' The next day crowds of volunteers came back to clean up the park. Huge piles of debris." Abramson left the Cleveland concert scene for other opportunities, but did so on a high note.

As it turned out, Musicarnival was starting to see its final days. The tent had to be replaced every few years, the summer heat could be brutal, and sirens from Warrensville Heights safety crews would often disrupt shows. If Musicarnival could be that successful with midsize shows in the summer months, why couldn't the season be expanded with a permanent building? Highland Heights was chosen for a 3,000 seat theater-in-the-round off Wilson Mills Road. At first there would be a 26-week season aimed at the Tom Jones–Engelbert Humperdinck–Sonny and Cher crowd, though any act that could fill the hall would be welcome. It was right off Interstate 271 and promised serious tax revenue for the city. John Price at Musicarnival said he wasn't worried. The land was owned by the DeBartolo family, who were building the giant Randall Park Mall down the street. Price said there had even been talk about moving Musicarnival to the mall, and there was an option to move the operation to a permanent structure. In reality, he was whistling past the graveyard.

On July 5, 1974, the Front Row Theater had a gala opening, a first-night fund-raiser with elegant parties and a black-tie crowd. Sammy Davis Jr. was the first headliner and he settled in for a two-week stay, and there was a long line of guests waiting for their turn on the revolving stage. The Jackson Five was there in the first month, and rock acts started booking the new theater. Chuck Berry and Little Richard packed the house long after the Musicarnival season had ended, and plenty of other stars were set for the winter. Years later, Roy Orbison would play his last live show there. The writing was on the wall for the big tent.

The competition was simply overwhelming, and Musicarnival announced that the 1975 season would be its last. The Front Row had 700 more seats than the tent, which meant it could bid higher for top acts. Besides the Front Row, you now had the Coliseum in Richfield, and the Cleveland Agora was booking rock acts weekly. The tent poles came down for the last time in mid-August 1975.

Musicarnival thrived when it lured acts away from the dying Playhouse Square of the late 1960s. The Front Row booked acts for 19 years until it fell to competition from resurrected Playhouse Square theaters. What goes around comes around.

Euclid Tavern

11625 Euclid Avenue, Cleveland

Some cleveland-area bars have been around forever, but you don't hear a lot about them. Folks may want to keep them neighborhood secrets because they like it that way. The Euclid Tavern had been around for almost a century, but it wasn't until the 1990s that people started hearing the big noise that drew from all over Northeast Ohio.

"The Euc" always drew respectable crowds; you don't stay in business if you don't. But many came from colleges, and that crowd keeps changing. The tavern had a unique way of doing business: It was very casual. Story was that regulars would go behind the bar and serve themselves, and the owners trusted you to pay for what you drank. Every now and then the bar would generate some headlines. In 1986, director Paul Schrader shot scenes for the film *Light of Day* with Joan Jett and other musicians at the Euc. But you need people coming through the door regularly. Monday nights at just about any bar are deadly. Sports bars cash in on big games, but if nothing is happening on-screen it's not happening in your bar either. So what to do? Music is the universal language.

Paul DeVito, Bob Jost, and Jimmy Cvelbar were in charge. They had a guy in the kitchen named Jerry Suhar who played guitar, and they asked him to leave the grill and hit the stage. This was back in 1980, and Suhar settled in for a long stay doing his weekly open mic night. It worked for about 10 years, but remember what we said about the changing crowd.

Then, in walked a former patron who used to tear up the place before he left for Detroit: Derek Hess.

"I was living in Cleveland," Hess says. "I was really bad, across the board. Bad in school. Bad out of school. A bad dude! Then I moved to Detroit, which is BAD! It was a bad idea! But I got my act together in Detroit and moved back to Cleveland. I came back and studied art again, but I needed a job. My watering hole before I left for Detroit was the Euclid Tavern, so I knew all of them. We were tight, but I came back sober and asked for a job. They thought about it and said, 'You can chop chicken wings for wing night!' I would go down in the basement and there would be 14 to 20 40-pound cases of chicken wings that had to be chopped up before the frat boys showed up."

Hess realized early on there was no real future in chicken wing nights for either him or the chickens, but a light went on after a talk with the owners.

"They were complaining about how bad their Monday nights were," Hess recalls. "It was CIA [Cleveland Institute of Art] night, and students used to come, but times change, people graduate and the new ones weren't coming in. I had seen all these bands in Detroit that were skipping the Cleveland market due to promoters and logistics and whatnot. Some had played venues here where they weren't getting the deals they were guaranteed, so the agents and bands started to skip Cleveland. They made it a travel day and drove to Buffalo or Detroit. I said, 'Why don't we get these bands I was seeing in Detroit? Let's get them here to play the Euclid Tavern.' I kept bugging them and then, one day, the owner said, 'Well why don't you do this? Why don't you get the bands?' I always said if I was ever in the place where I could make a difference musically, I would do it. I was given an opportunity.

"It was local bands initially," Hess says. "Integrity was one of my first shows, and I think Face Value was with them. They were notorious for pissing people off. That was their thing. Straight-edge. Drinking booze. They hate you. They came in, they set up, they played and they were out of there by 11. The owners are looking at me with their jaws dropped saying, 'What in the hell did you just do to us?! Not a soul bought a beer, it's only 11 o'clock and we're

One of the oldest bars in Cleveland, the Euclid Tavern (shown here in 1982) drew a loyal clientele from local colleges thanks to inexpensive drinks and shows by up-and-coming rock bands. *(Cleveland Public Library)*

open.' I was, like, 'Hey. I'll do better!'" If he didn't he was back to whacking chicken wings, and that got old pretty quick.

"I started looking around and getting bands like Starvation Army and Prisonshake. There were the Burning Lesbians, and some of them became Dimbulb. The Vivians played there a few times. The drinks started flowing." Hess tells us drinks can get emotions flowing, too. Anything can happen in a bar, and when it does you have to act fast. "There was a big fight at one of these shows. I had a band from the east side and a band from the west side, and the band from the west side were Nazis. I didn't know this. The guys from the east side weren't liberal but they sure weren't Nazis. If anything, they were anti-Nazis. This huge fight broke out and these guys were monsters. Me and Bob Jost, one of the owners, are standing in the middle of this circle. Bob's holding a billy club and I've got his back, and Bob says, 'Who do we hit first?' I said, 'I don't know, Bob. The police are here. Let them handle it.' Eleven squad cars showed up and they cleared the room.

I knew the next day the owners were going to have a talk with me about booking shows there, so I filled my calendar that night when I got home. The next day, sure enough, they called me in and it was like, 'Well, why don't we just play out what you have in the calendar. We'll see how it goes.' Never had a real problem after that. It was all a learning experience."

It's hard to argue with success, Hess says.

"We did really, really well with the local stuff, and I got a tip about this band Helmet. They were new on Amphetamine Reptile Records, and they were coming through from New York. They needed a gig. A friend who used to work at the Agora told me, 'Derek, don't book music if you like it.' Why is that? 'Cause then you'll give them too much money!' The agent heard my voice. 'Helmet! Really! How much?' And then it was like he was reeling me in. He knew that he had a sucker. I broke even. I didn't lose money, but I didn't make any and I could have if I was a little more shrewd as I learned to be a little later on. It was their first national gig at the Euclid Tavern and I did what you're supposed to do. I paid the band and gave them their beer. What's so hard about that?" Doesn't seem hard at all, and Hess says bands remember a good time.

"Helmet came back for a second time on that same tour and they came with Jawbox, and Jawbox was exploding. They wanted to play another room but Helmet was, like, 'No! We love the Euclid Tavern' and at this point all the agents were starting to love the Euclid Tavern. An agent will handle a bunch of bands, and if you treat the agent well he'll send you all their bands. I was getting all the Amphetamine bands, I was getting all the Touch and Go bands. All the Sub Pop bands. When we had Jawbox with Helmet we must have 400 people in that room. It was ridiculous." Such a bill builds loyalty with the bands and the audience.

"Cop Shoot Cop almost became a house band. Cop Shoot Cop, Jesus Lizard, and the Cows were all out-of-town bands. There was Tar, from Chicago, too. I would call them up when I needed them, see if they would do a one-off, and most of the time they could.

They loved the room, the agents loved the room, and Cop Shoot Cop had their best show ever there." That band also drew some unique fans. "I had these two guys in there from the art school, and we just had a local band on. Maybe 20 people there. These two guys are big, big sculpture artists or whatever the hell they did, and they decide they want to start waltzing. They're going around the center of the dance floor. Swinging around and knocking people over. I'm looking at them like, 'How am I going to bounce these guys? I wouldn't have a chance.' So, what I did was I hired them. They were security from then on out.

"When Cop Shoot Cop played their first date they didn't know what to expect, but we had a real good vibe. A good energy about it because we hyped it big. I had all the college radio stations playing hot on Cop Shoot Cop. The place filled up and people just went off. Hanging off the rafters. The singer is getting the mic bashed into his mouth and he's bleeding. I told the guys, 'Dudes! You gotta get up there and hold up those mics. I don't care how many people are going to pile on your back. We gotta make this happen.' Sure enough, they took it, and Cop Shoot Cop fell in love with us and would do one-offs. Jesus Lizard as well, though we didn't have to do that with them. They were attacking the crowd."

The city's rock and roll reputation grew stronger with the Euc. In the summer of 1995, the owners gave Hess a challenge. For the opening of the Rock and Roll Hall of Fame, there would be three nights of festivities downtown.

"The owners of the tavern said, 'We need something to cover three nights at the Euc.' I called the agent for Jesus Lizard. They filled the house all three nights while all the other festivities were going on in downtown Cleveland. Every time there was a break in between songs, David Yow would yell out something like, 'Ladies and gentlemen . . . Mr. Bruce Springsteen!' He would point at the door and everyone is looking around. 'Mr. Phil Collins!' Same thing every time."

Once, Hess was put in the position of *not* promoting someone.

"We booked Sean Lennon at the Euc. He was with this band

Cibo Matto. It was him, someone from Jon Spencer—it may have even been Jon Spencer—and the two Asian girls, and I was not allowed to promote that Sean Lennon would be there. That was a no-no. Even so, it got whispered around a little bit."

Cibo Matto had their own demands, too.

"The bookers get a rider. A rider is what you supply the band with in their contract. What kind of beer, what kind of food, what kind of dressing room. We didn't have a dressing room at the Euc. They always wanted a certain kind of tea with a certain kind of honey. All right, so I go running around all over Cleveland and I find the tea and I find the honey. We made them a little space and they didn't touch the honey. They were so cute you couldn't be mad at them. They filled the room, so okay. They come around the next year, I get the rider and it's the same thing, but I saved the honey. They never used it."

Sometimes, those riders were a challenge.

"I had the Melvins in. They rattled the clock off the wall with their opening note. It was pretty impressive. They wanted in their Jolt Cola. That was before all these energy drinks. It was just caffeine. It was on its way out, so it was hard to find. I drove all over the city looking for Jolt Cola but I got it. I was talking to them about how the night was going to go, and they're veterans. It was like, 'Yeah, kid. We know what we're doing.' You go on at this time, I'll have my dudes holding the speakers up, blah blah blah. All of a sudden my sound man puts on Kiss, 'Strutter.' They just tuned me out. Soon as that first drum hit they started doing air drums and weren't even looking at me anymore. I was not there. They were the biggest Kiss fans so I just walked away. You guys get it."

Hess says some bands tend to work on their own schedules, too, which makes club owners nervous. One was Surgery, from New York City.

"They were cool," Hess says. "New York cool. I'm waiting on them, and I'm becoming the nervous promoter. I'm on the phone with their agent, and he's telling me, 'Oh, they said they'd be there.' Well, I have to put the opening band on and I don't have a head-

Derek Hess got a job at the Euclid Tavern prepping chicken in the basement for Wing Night. He moved up to booking bands, making fliers, and eventually creating posters in his distinctive style—some of which are now in major museum collections. *(Derek Hess)*

liner. It's getting really late. Finally, one of my regulars comes running in and says, 'There's a van parked on the sidewalk by the load in door.' Good! The band's here. I walk out to the van, I knock on the glass and they're not looking at me. They roll down the window and the cloud of reefer comes out. 'You the band?' 'Uh . . . yeah.' I asked if they wanted to load in. 'Yeah. Load in. In a minute.' Cool. I walked back to the front door, they open their van door and it was stereotypical Spinal Tap. The door opens and beer cans fall out. But hey, they made it and they were very good."

So how were people finding out about these bands? That became an opportunity for Derek Hess, too. "I was studying print-making at the time and making fliers for all my shows. I was my own client, so I could do whatever I wanted with these fliers. Same thing with posters. We were flier maniacs. We knew which poles to target and then we would go back and hit them again."

What about sure draws where the Euc took a pass? Hess has one that comes to mind right away, and no regrets.

"G.G. Allin wanted to play the Euclid Tavern. He was the nastiest of the nasty punk rockers. When I lived in Detroit, I was working security at my building and I couldn't go to his show, but my punk rocker buddy told me, 'G.G. Allin just rolled around and opened up his bowels and it all came out! Then he ran up and grabbed pitchers of beer from some skinheads and he started beating himself with the pitchers and he's doing all this crazy stuff.' No way he's playing the Euc. He would fill the house, but who's cleaning that up? The rumor was he was going to kill himself onstage, and I said if I could get it in the contract that G.G. Allin would kill himself at the Euclid Tavern we'll do the show. Now that would go down in punk rock history." Fortunately, that contract was never signed.

The big draws still loved coming to the Euc even after they hit the major leagues.

"Soul Coughing came through once, opening for Cop Shoot Cop. There was a big buzz on Soul Coughing through *Alternative Press* magazine. They came on and they were amazing. Everyone stayed for Cop Shoot Cop, but immediately after they [Soul Coughing] were headliners and very loyal to the Euclid Tavern. They opened for Dave Matthews at the Gund Arena, and they said, 'As soon as we're done here we're heading over to the Euclid Tavern to do a show.' They shot over and gave a show. They would do secret shows, just word-of-mouth, and take whatever we got at the door. Once I had them there with a packed house and a long line outside waiting to get in. I told my security guys to walk around the room and find some underage drinkers so we can throw them out."

Oh, and you didn't want to get thrown out.

"We had a special way to bounce people, too. You got a hold of them and rammed them into the cigarette machine. Then you pushed them through the door of the vestibule and into the wall. You bring them back through that door to the phone booth door and crash them into that. Then you take them back through the vestibule and you trip them so they go down on the ground. No one really got hurt bad, and it made a lot of noise. We just wanted to make a lot of noise. It made a point."

The booze wasn't always the only reason to keep an eye on the crowd.

"Oroboros—that was often a pot-smoking crowd. My job was not to stop the pot. My job was to walk around and make these hippies put their shoes on. They were 'earth whirlers.' They take their shoes off and dance around like they're at Woodstock. I'm like, 'There's glass on the floor. Put the shoes on!'"

Hess eventually moved on, and the owners sold the Euc in the late 1990s. The tavern closed for a time, reopened under new management, and closed again in 2018, but was never again like it was during its heyday.

As for Derek Hess, the guy who stapled fliers to telephone poles: His career took off and you can see his artwork everywhere, including the Louvre! No staple marks, either.

Cleveland Public Auditorium

500 Lakeside Avenue, Cleveland

No discussion of northeast Ohio's rock venues is complete without mention of Cleveland's Public Auditorium, which most people just call Public Hall. Before the Richfield Coliseum opened for business, it was the biggest concert stage in town under one roof. Hundreds of acts performed there, and there's no way to comment on all of them here, but let's touch on some of the highlights the auditorium—and the Music Hall, next door—have seen over the years.

First, it's old. Public Hall opened in 1922, when commercial radio had been around for just a couple of years. Its architects never anticipated the kind of mayhem that rock concerts would bring. For the first 50 years or so, patrons could smoke in the hall, and in the rock years people smoked just about everything. Sound engineering was nowhere near as sophisticated as it is today, and over the years groups played louder and louder, creating issues. It was a place meant for conventions and trade shows. There were plenty of those, and lots of folks came out for the annual food show, the Home and Flower Show, and the Sportsmen's Show.

A new era began in September 1964.

Cleveland was a dull and gray place after the assassination of President Kennedy. There was worldwide mourning, we were dealing with the Cold War, the struggle for civil rights was unfolding, the space race was on, and people were questioning why the U.S. was in Viet Nam. Besides, Northeast Ohio was fighting a really tough winter. Then, in February 1964, the Beatles appeared on the *Ed Sullivan Show*, and, as Keith Richards is credited with saying, "The world was in color again."

Cleveland's Public Auditorium, commonly referred to as Public Hall, showcased everything from food shows to political conventions. But no one expected the mayhem created when Beatlemania roared into town.
(Cleveland Press Collection, Cleveland State University Archives)

The Beatles breathed new life into pop music and Top 40 radio. KYW and WHK were the big dogs in Northeast Ohio, and Norm Wain, Bob Weiss, and Joe Zingale (who would go on to start WIXY 1260) were the premier sales team at WHK. They saw the promotional value in landing the Fab Four, and started working the phones. The Beatles had planned to bypass Cleveland, but that meant nothing to these three. MCA was booking the tour, and there was an open date. The agency said KYW was trying to land the show, too. Whoever booked Public Hall first got the bragging rights. Those were the days when a handshake was just about as good as a contract, and WHK got a preliminary okay. Zingale flew to New York City for talks with Beatles manager Brian Epstein and the folks at MCA. Keep in mind that KYW was 50,000 watts and was not happy to have the rug pulled out from under it. Its people were making calls, too.

Zingale called back to Cleveland and said MCA wanted something in writing affirming that WHK had the convention center. That was easy enough. Either Wain or Weiss sent a phony telegram with a signature from the hall's manager and 'HK had a lock on the Beatles. The date was September 15.

When the Beatles toured the U.S. in 1964, they saw the hotel, the venue, the hotel, the venue . . . There was very little time for sight-seeing, and it was no different in Cleveland. All came down to security. Mobs of young people gathered outside the Sheraton-Cleveland on Public Square, meaning the band would go nowhere without a police escort. Media was called to the hotel for a press conference and the Beatles got the usual questions about screaming girls and haircuts. But one reporter asked if the band was going to meet with Ghoulardi. Who? The reporter said (mistakenly) that local late-night TV host Ghoulardi "was the first to play your records." John Lennon asked if he really was, because a lot of people were making that claim, and Paul McCartney added that if he actually was, he had good taste. After a bite to eat, it was off to the show.

It cannot be stressed enough that the city had never experienced a show like the one that night at Public Hall, and Cleveland Police weren't really sure how to handle it. It was a five-act bill with the Bill Black Combo, The Exciters, Clarence "Frogman" Henry, and Jackie DeShannon, but the place exploded when the Beatles hit the stage. Sinatra, Elvis—no one had ever gotten a reaction like the Fab Four, and the crowd screamed louder and louder as the show went on. You couldn't hear the music; some kids looked like they were having seizures, and then there were the jelly beans. Those damned jelly beans! A few weeks before, George Harrison had mentioned how much he liked jelly babies, which are softer than American candy, but you still feel them when they hit, and boy, did they get hit. Thousands rained down at every show, and Cleveland was no different. They also hit policemen.

Plain Dealer reporter Don Robertson was at the show, and he said it bordered on mob violence. Police cordoned off the stage to hold back the crowds and, at first, the cops were losing. One girl fainted, another got trampled, and both needed medical attention at the scene. At that point, Carl Bare, the police deputy inspector, stopped the concert, yelling "this show is over"—though the Beatles were still playing. That didn't sit well with the band. Lennon made a face at Bare and did a little dance, and the crowd started getting angry. Bare gave the crowd an angry look, and then crossed the imaginary red line. He pulled Harrison's guitar cord out of his amplifier, and you didn't touch a Beatle or his equipment. Harrison was fuming and took steps toward Bare, but was hurried off the stage. One witness thought Harrison would take a swing at Bare, which would have really set off the powder keg.

There were 500 policemen on duty, but 10,000-plus Beatle fans. The odds were not in favor of the cops, and there was a serious chance that someone was going to get hurt. Another inspector, "Iron Mike" Blackwell, stood with Bare as the giant curtain came down. Finally, after a few minutes Sergeant Edwin Nagorski came to the mic and hinted the show might continue saying, "You can yell all you want, but you have to stay seated!" and Beatles publicist Derek Taylor backed him up. Pretty soon the crowd started chanting, "Don't stand up! Don't stand up!," they brought up the curtain and the show resumed. That didn't keep people from throwing debris at the stage including a purse, a shoe, hairbrushes, combs, and streamers of toilet paper rolls.

There were also reports of gangs of kids breaking windows to get backstage through the Music Hall, with even more trying to get in through basement windows. Another 500 were at the stage door on East 6th Street, and they were far from quiet. Police had their hands full trying to break up the crowd. Then the crowd spotted Dick Goddard, who at the time was with KYW, and the police had to rescue him, too. The Beatles had a chartered jet waiting at Hopkins Airport, and the band was smuggled out with no problems. But a bus that was being used to transport the rest

Cleveland's finest lined the stage to keep over-enthusiastic fans from rushing the
Beatles during their 1964 performance at Public Auditorium. *(George Shuba)*

of the Beatles entourage got stuck in the nearby mall garage and
the plane had to wait another 90 minutes until a new bus arrived.
It was off to New Orleans. What a night.

The next day, Public Hall's maintenance crew noticed something different during cleanup. There was no problem sweeping up
the trash, but there was something in the air. It was strong, too. It
was the smell of urine. This aroma turned up at most of the shows.
People didn't want to leave their seats because they feared they
wouldn't be able to get back, and then some of them lost control
during the show. People were talking about the show for days, and
not everyone was happy. Promoters had already booked Public
Hall for more British Invasion acts, and the city wasn't about to
do this week after week.

The city started adding up the numbers. Three people were seriously hurt at the concert, including a girl who beat her head against

Police formed a human barricade to keep the crowds back while the Beatles performed. *(George Shuba)*

a cement wall. Paul Hurd, the commissioner for both Public Hall and Municipal Stadium, said he had never seen such a mountain of trash in his 19 years on the job. Doors were twisted out of shape, with some pulled off their hinges, adding a $500 repair bill to the $2,300 WHK paid to rent the hall.

Then the Beatles camp chimed in. Lennon said that Cleveland show "was the least wild of all of the American shows, the most calm show we ever played. That was the amazing thing. The kids were quieter there than anywhere. They didn't warrant the police." Ringo Starr went so far as to call the cops "stupid," and Harrison had choice words for Inspector Bare. Publicist Derek Taylor said the police failed to keep back the crowds, and some were bugging the band for autographs. "The police were unable to cope," he said. "They had too many men at the hotel and not enough at the hall."

In fact, a *Cleveland Press* photo showed a teenage girl doubled over, supposedly emotionally overwrought by the Beatles appearance. But years later, that same teenager, by then an adult, claimed she and others alongside her were roughed up by cops with billy clubs. But a police spokesman said the band started it all, getting the crowds riled up by waving at them at the hotel, and on top of that they were "unwashed and smelly."

The post-mortem continued with an analysis by a Western Reserve University psychologist who said that a lot of the problems could have been avoided. "Those WHK disc jockeys whipped up those children to a frenzy," the psychologist said. "At the airport Monday night, for instance, the children were behaving themselves nicely—until the disc jockeys began yelling at them. And, of course, all the news coverage didn't help. It made them all want to perform." Was it some kind of sexual attraction? Nah! The psychologist said that "with those hairdos, the Beatles are essentially sexless!"

Some good came out of the experience. A philanthropic organization, the Variety Club, joined with theater owners around Northeast Ohio to fund Ohio Boys Town by selling carpeting from the room the Beatles occupied at the Sheraton-Cleveland. They cut up 90,720 pieces in hopes of raising nearly $100,000 at a buck apiece. If you showed up at the Mapletown, Olympia, Variety, or 21 other local theaters for a special Saturday matinee in October, you got a one-inch square and a certificate of authenticity.

Nevertheless, the city still had an axe to grind.

Mayor Ralph Locher saw the headlines and got an earful from the police unions. These music groups made people act weird and they looked funny, too. Back in those days boys had "butch" haircuts or maybe a flat-top. When they got older they might switch to a snappy New Yorker, flat on top and swept back on the sides. Cleveland didn't need guys who couldn't see their eyebrows coming in and riling up the kids. Juvenile Court Judge Angelo Gagliardo said concerts of that type "were like feeding narcotics to teenagers." He called them "dangerous and could well lead to riots." A promoter from Chicago named Ed Pazdur had booked Public Hall for two shows, and the city had to honor its contracts, but after that, forget it. Locher ordered that no publicly owned facility would be used for shows of that type. Circuses and trade shows were a lot more productive and orderly. Who needs a Beatle when you can see a chimp ride a bicycle? Now that's entertainment!

About six weeks after the Beatles show, the city braced for the Cleveland debut of the Rolling Stones. The Stones were seen as the Fab Four's main competition, but you wouldn't know it by comparing the two Public Hall shows. On November 3rd, the Stones arrived on stage before a thousand people, one-tenth of what the Beatles drew, and Mick Jagger and crew were furious. Most of the audience was very young teenage girls who came to scream, and the *Plain Dealer* called the show "a flop." Even so, plenty of people took risks and got hurt, giving Mayor Locher more ammunition. A 17-year old girl fell 20 feet from a balcony, and a bunch of girls rushed the stage when the Stones appeared. Cops started throwing girls off the stage or grabbing them by the ankles, shoving kids who even looked like they would do something. This was a smaller crowd than the Beatles' but no less energetic, but that was no consolation to the band or its sponsors.

A few other factors affected the crowd size. There was a snow-storm that night, a presidential election with two controversial candidates was in process, and some parents wouldn't let their kids go even if they had tickets. Scott Burton was WHK's program director. He blamed the judge and the mayor, and the promoter, Pazdur, demanded a public apology. The Stones? They hated playing to a small house with pockets of empty seats. When the press showed up at their suite at the Statler Hotel after the show, doors slammed in their faces. One show left. The outlook for rock and roll shows in Cleveland was not good.

Another six weeks went by and it was time for the Dave Clark Five, the band had that played the *Ed Sullivan Show* the week after the Beatles. They weren't scruffy like the Rolling Stones—they dressed in matching suits—and it was hoped there would be no trouble. Pazdur hired extra security people described as "prime beef males" to line the front of the stage. The crowd was bigger, about 3,000 seats, but he was still expecting a $4,000 loss for the night. Even so, there was something different. Kids yelled but they stayed in their seats, and if they stood up or looked like they were ready to make a run, an usher would whisper in their ear and they sat back down. That show may have turned around public opinion. The ban was eventually lifted, and rock bands had access to a big hall on the shores of Lake Erie.

Public Auditorium welcomed a long line of show business legends. Judy Garland, Johnny Carson. Harry Belafonte and Aretha Franklin opening for Dr. Martin Luther King Jr. Those shows were easily managed. But with rock acts, anything could happen and usually did: The Monkees drove a teenage audience into a frenzy when they appeared in January 1967. Five people were injured, and the band's production company, Screen Gems, ended up paying hundreds of dollars in damages for the hall.

1968 was a huge year for the complex. Simon and Garfunkel packed the hall, and Blood, Sweat & Tears opened for Janis Joplin, who took the stage swinging a bottle of Southern Comfort. Jimi Hendrix played back-to-back shows at the Music Hall next door. And then there were the Doors. Lead singer Jim Morrison showed up drunk and late following an afternoon at Cleveland watering holes. He stumbled onto the stage, his head jerking from side to side, and started goading the audience. At one point, he jumped into the audience and was thrown back toward the band. It wasn't long before the crowd got ugly, and police charged back, generating a small riot. Footage of that clash would be used years later in a Doors video for "Roadhouse Blues." The video was produced in the 1980s to take advantage of early MTV. It shows cops knocking heads under a clock on the main floor of the auditorium. Oddly enough, that clock was broken back in 1968 and stayed that way even after the video was released.

Within three years of their Cleveland appearances Joplin, Hendrix, and Morrison would all be dead, victims of their own excess.

WIXY 1260 promoted shows including a 1969 bill that featured Neil Diamond, Tommy James and the Shondells, Bob Seger, Canned Heat, and Kenny Rogers. WIXY was known for its eclectic lineups!

Led Zeppelin had made a huge impact in the few months following its 1969 Cleveland-area debut at Musicarnival. They were booked the same year at Public Hall, an October 24 date with Grand Funk Railroad opening, and with a bit of a twist: It was announced that there would be no seating on the main floor. Bring a blanket or pillow to sit on, and feel free to dance if you want, because the only chairs would be in the balcony. This sort of arrangement would lead to the Who tragedy in Cincinnati in 1979 and was pretty common up to that time.

Another issue had to be dealt with before the show. Belkin Productions had gotten word that Zep bassist John Paul Jones, because of a family emergency, had to leave for London. The tour would be temporarily suspended after the Cleveland show—which now had to start three hours early in order for Jones to make the flight home. The Belkins took out newspaper ads and radio spots to get the word out, offering refunds to those who couldn't make the earlier time.

Steve Sinton, who used the air name Ginger Sutton on WNCR, remembers sitting in the back of a limo with the band after the show. "It was club seating. The rear seats faced each other. I'm face-to-face with Robert Plant. He's next to John Bonham and Jimmy Page.

"John Paul Jones' grandfather died in Scotland, and he had to catch an evening plane back for the service, so Zeppelin moved the show up to 5:30 p.m.—and got a half-full room to show for it. Jones did the set, but split before the encore. The band asked for a volunteer from the audience to play bass, and the first kid out of a hundred to get to the stage did. He helped them with three songs, all of them wooden, from the brand new Led Zeppelin III album."

The scene after the show was almost surreal.

"Bonham was calm and quiet as drummers are right after a

Moon shot: The Who's Keith Moon often targeted security in front of the stage with well-aimed drumsticks. When the guards turned around to see where the blow came from, Moon already had another stick in his hand, and never missed a beat. *(George Shuba)*

gig. Jimmy had recently cut his hair short and grown a beard and was in the throes of Guinness Book heroin addiction. He barely opened his eyes all night, including on stage. They're all 26. I'm 19. I learned in the back of the car that the world revolves around Robert Plant."

How so? "He was upset about the light turnout, but made it all about Jones. 'How could something as personal as a family death be made so public?' He was referring to the discussion of Jones' grandfather's death on our radio station and by Jane Scott in the *Plain Dealer*."

"I told him, 'Robert, 13,000 people had tickets for this gig. Half of them couldn't leave work in time to see it. You have to give them a reason why.' He kept grumbling all the way back to the Hollenden House.

"When people ask me who the most egotistical performer I ever met was, I name Bob." Was there anything positive about the ride back? "The limo was a Chrysler Imperial. I'd love to have that car now."

Hindsight is 20/20, but some of the shows might have been better thought out. July 1971 saw hard-rocking Sweathog open for headliner Black Sabbath. Sandwiched in between was the folk act Brewer & Shipley, riding the wave of their hit, "One Toke Over the Line." Not a good mix, especially considering the abundance of fireworks tossed on stage.

Still, there were plenty of memorable shows. When the Who came on August 12, 1971, promoting *Who's Next*, Keith Moon ran out in his underwear with a small plastic trash bin full of drumsticks under his arm. In those days, promoters sometimes hired martial arts experts to line the front of the stage, and with the crazy drugs going around there was no shortage of people trying to jump on the stage. They had their hands full keeping them off, but when Moon spotted someone getting roughed up he would throw a drumstick with amazing accuracy. What's more amazing is that the guard would spin around and see Moon drumming away with two sticks and a big grin. He never missed a beat!

Cleveland held its own as a concert town despite its economic instability, but three shows in late 1972 cemented its reputation. Concerned about the amount of Southern rock it was playing (Allman Brothers, Wet Willie, and others), WMMS heavily promoted David Bowie's *Hunky Dory* LP. Bowie was planning an autumn tour to promote his new album *The Rise and Fall of Ziggy Stardust and the Spiders from Mars*, he had radio support in Cleveland as well as a fan club, and Music Hall looked as good a place as any to start a tour.

The concert sold out in days, and no one was really sure what to expect. Some fans came dressed as droogs from the movie *A Clockwork Orange*, others arrived in homemade space gear, but none could match Bowie himself. Razor-cut hair, no eyebrows and scary thin. The show was a triumph, and the station must have been very confident it would be. As they entered the hall, fans found stickers advertising a November show at Public Hall. That turned into two sold-out shows, even though Bowie was getting mixed response in many of the cities he played. Bowie never forgot Cleveland or WMMS.

Bowie would play Public Hall several more times, as would a wide range of acts including Queen on Valentine's Day 1976, Electric Light Orchestra the following year, and Van Halen for two nights in 1979. Many of the bigger shows would move to the Richfield Coliseum, but the music world came full circle when Cleveland won the Rock and Roll Hall of Fame. After some time, the yearly inductions have come to be staged in Cleveland on a regular basis at what seemed the most logical choice: Cleveland's Public Auditorium.

Phantasy Nite Club and Theater

11794 to 11814 Detroit Avenue, Lakewood

EVERY CLEVELAND AREA ROCK venue has its own personality, but the Phantasy Entertainment Complex is the only one with a pirate ship. Besides the ship, there's a lot more to cover in a building that houses the Phantasy Nite Club, Theater, Chamber, and Symposium. The heritage goes all the way back to 1918 when neighborhood theaters were as busy as the corner bar. The Homestead Theater opened at that site and was a movie house until 1979. It had several names along the way including the Detroit Theater and the Last Picture Show, and there was even an eatery when John DeFrasia took over the building in 1965 and opened the Piccadilly Square restaurant.

Now, about that ship. It was created using a steam furnace to bend white-oak wood and metal and held 7,000 screws. DeFrasia cut the ship in half when Piccadilly Square was transformed into a music venue. Michele DeFrasia knows the ship well. "It is an actual half-scale replica of the H.M.S. Bounty from the movie *Mutiny On The Bounty* that starred Marlon Brando. My father had a Canadian shipbuilder come in and build the ship inside the club. All of the rigging was done in the Cleveland ship yards. He had many a captain marry couples on her."

Michele says her dad didn't consider adding more boats, though she has "all of the copies of the original plans, which included two other ships as well." When the complex was renamed the Phantasy in the early 1980s, the ship saw use as a DJ booth and sound stage. So how did it evolve from the Piccadilly to the Phantasy? "It just fell into that groove," she says. "The club was being booked by Bart Koster back in the late '70s; then he moved on and I took over booking in 1980. Then Jim O'Brian came into the picture and decided to open the Homestead Theater and renamed it The Phantasy Theater. He got a group of people to come in and all work together and open the theater in 1982, with our first show being The Psychedelic Furs. Eventually we started booking our own shows—the Thompson Twins, Oingo Boingo, and Ministry, just to name a few. Then Belkin Productions started booking shows in the theater, and after that House of Blues was doing its shows in the theater till they opened HOB downtown."

Hank Berger named and opened The Phantasy Nite Club back in the 1970s. Alt and goth bands found a welcome home at the club, and the FM college radio stations helped promote big-time. Cleveland State's WCSB, WRUW at Case Western Reserve, John Carroll had WUJC, Baldwin Wallace had WBWC, and WOBC at Oberlin College brought out the crowds. Michele also had close ties with the record labels, but that could mean extra work. "They would have numerous release parties for bands. The Cure was one of them off the top of my head for *Blood Flowers*. They gave away dead roses at the door, but we had to take off all of the thorns before we could open the doors."

Local bands got a break at the Phantasy, too. If they had a following they could open for some of the national acts that played there. After a time, Michele says, "The nationals started bringing their own bands on tour with them. Most of the time the opening out-of-town bands were represented by the same agents as the main band." Even so, the locals had plenty of work there with acts like the Exotic Birds, Odd Girl Out, the Generators, the Adults getting some great exposure. It also opened the door for the industrial music scene. Michele recalls, "That's around when the Chamber, our Goth club, opened. Trent Reznor's Nine Inch Nails used that as a rehearsal space as well for their upcoming tours."

Reznor had other links to the Phantasy complex.

Success in the music industry is based on relationships, and Michele says the Phantasy was a great place to network. "When Skinny Puppy performed in the Theater, Trent Reznor was at the

Actor Michael J. Fox made a surprise appearance at the Phantasy to trade licks with Joan Jett and her band. The two filmed the movie *Light of Day* in Cleveland. *(Janet Macoska)*

show, and I introduced him to the band. They immediately wanted Reznor and his band on one of their tour dates, maybe more; I can't remember. Reznor started his Nine Inch Nails career up in the Phantasy, so it was his home club. NIN started rehearsing in The Phantasy Nite Club and The Theater and performing there as well. In fact, John Malm Jr. met Reznor at the Phantasy Nite Club. Reznor was in a local cover band called I think, The Hurt. After they met they started working together and developed the group NIN. Malm was a major factor in Reznor's success, from the music to the artwork to picking out the video directors for many of his biggest songs. Rich Patrick started his career at the Phantasy Nite Club with his band the AKT." The two ended up in one of the early versions of Nine Inch Nails.

Actors known for a particular role can be stereotyped and that can mean curtains for their career. The same thing can happen with clubs, and the Phantasy catered to a special audience. The DeFrasias weren't worried. "I had no concerns about our club having a niche audience because it did very well for us and I really liked the music and the people. It eventually led to other styles of music for us to investigate and book, [like] the metal and punk scene as well as the '80s hair scene. We had started a very successful '80s night during that decade. We would feature different DJs from various local college radio stations as well as musicians who were in town and would stop by and spin a few discs. For example, Matt Johnson from The The. A lot of the local musicians would be guest DJs, like Andy Kubiszewski, lead vocalist with Exotic Birds. He was one of our regular Thursday Nite DJs, and eventually went on to perform in Stabbing Westward. Now he does TV sound tracks for *Ice Road Truckers, Storage Wars* and other shows."

The Phantasy was very much a DeFrasia family operation. As Michele tells it, "We all worked and we all had our jobs. Whether it was an outside promoter or our own show we worked together." That also meant dealing with the artists. "Iggy Pop! My father was going to kick him out of the upstairs kitchen and out of the building. Iggy kept gargling and spitting in the kitchen sink. He wouldn't stop, so my dad was bound and determined to kick him out. But the show went on, thank God."

The kitchen loomed large.

"The Red Hot Chili Peppers were late getting on stage in the Theater. My mom had Flea cleaning up his mess in the kitchen before he was allowed to go down to the Theater to perform. He had cut someone's hair and was going to leave the mess." Then there was a night in 1987 before the premiere of a movie filmed in Cleveland. The movie was *Light of Day,* and one of the stars, Michael J. Fox, stopped by for a surprise walk-on to play with Joan Jett and the Blackhearts. "I ran into Michael in the back upstairs band room and he thought I was Joan Jett," Michele recalls. "He picked me up and twirled me around in the air. I was like, 'Excuse me but I think you think I'm someone else.' He immediately put me down and said he was so sorry, he thought I was Joan. Then that same day, it was my little twin brother and sister's 16th birthday. I asked Michael to come in the kitchen so they could meet him and he picked up Maggie and gave her her first kiss on the cheek. That made her 16th birthday!"

Otherwise, however, club work can be just that: work.

"My whole family was involved to make each and every show a success," Michele says. "The Jesus and Mary Chain performed a few times in the theater. One that comes to mind was when [the *Plain Dealer*'s] Jane Scott was there with *People* magazine. They were doing a story on her. Well, the Jesus and Mary Chain went on late, had their backs to the audience the whole time and only did a 20-minute set. That was not a good evening." Then there was Anthrax. "The drummer was arrested before they went on stage! He walked outside to go to his tour bus and was arrested by the Lakewood Police with a beer in his hand. My dad had to go down with Michael Belkin and get him out of jail so he could perform with the band."

The weather fouled things up once. Michele recalls, "It was during the big drought in the summertime. We had Erasure booked at the Phantasy Theater and Andrew Tosh performing in The Phantasy Nite Club. Well, a storm came through and cracked open the roof to the point where we had a waterfall coming down on the stage. That was the first time a show was rained out inside the club, instead of outside, for the promoter. Then I went upstairs, I found Andrew Tosh, Peter Tosh's son, passed out onstage due to 'smoking,' if you know what I mean. I was so mad. He was supposed to perform."

When acts spill out onto the street with their, uh . . . antics . . . they can draw the attention of neighbors.

"As for the neighborhood, I really never had a problem that I can think of except for the music being too loud sometimes. A lot of times we would have after-show parties for the national acts upstairs in The Phantasy Nite Club or in our Goth Club, The Chamber. After the shows, the hangout for stage guys and everyone that worked the shows was in The Symposium. My sister Diane ran that and her jukebox was voted best Jukebox in Cleveland back then."

So who played the Phantasy? A better question might be what up-and-coming band in the 1980s and '90s didn't play there? Plenty of established acts, too. Just a few names: John Lydon [formerly Johnny Rotten of the Sex Pistols], Los Lobos, Concrete Blonde, Crowded House, Bodeans, Psychedelic Furs, Dead Boys, Bad English, Kevin McMahon with Lucky Pierre and later, Prick, a band that would tour with David Bowie and Nine Inch Nails.

When John Defrasia passed away in 2011, he left behind a huge part of Cleveland rock history, a 54,000-square-foot complex that survived mosh pits, a 2009 fire and, some will even say, ghosts. Four years after his passing, the Phantasy was put up for sale. Three liquor licenses, top-notch staging, sound and lighting, and potential for even better days ahead. That will be up to its owners, but the DeFrasias continue to run the operation until that occurs. "The Phantasy will be remembered for its great music, the ship, of course, and for being very, very supportive of the local Cleveland music scene—and as the home of Nine Inch Nails." What about the ship? "Not sure what will happen to the ship," says Michele, "but it stays as long as we are there."

Variety Theatre

11815 Lorain Avenue, Cleveland

GREAT MUSIC HAS BEEN made on both sides of the Cuyahoga River. Take the Variety Theatre, which opened in 1927 for vaudeville shows and movies. In those days, going to a theater was a special occasion. There were chandeliers and very ornate decorations and staging, and just sitting there was quite an experience. It was the centerpiece of the neighborhood. Cleveland councilwoman Dona Brady reminisced to the *Plain Dealer* about Sunday matinees and how the theater kept kids out of the balcony. It was a pretty big house, too—1,900 seats—but times and tastes change, and like a lot of other neighborhood movie houses, the Variety struggled in its later years to get people through the door. By the 1980s it was screening dollar movies.

The Variety wasn't alone. Keep in mind that the Playhouse Square theaters were set for demolition before a community campaign helped develop them into the largest theater district outside New York City. The Variety was still a theater rather than just a movie house, though the vaudeville stage hadn't been used for a while. Live music looked like a viable option. But what kind of music? The area wasn't that accessible to all parts of town, and there were much flashier venues for top acts to visit. Maybe, just maybe, it could be like the old Fillmore East. Rock was starting to look like a viable alternative.

Cleveland radio had made the city a breakout market, with a huge influx of rock acts looking to play in Northeast Ohio. Plus, punk bands were getting a lot of air time from college radio stations that also sponsored the shows. Punk and post-punk had a solid audience thanks to Cleveland State's WCSB and WRUW at

Case Western Reserve, and metal had a big audience with jocks Bill Peters and Mario Becerra at John Carroll's WUJC (now WJCU). A growing number of MTV-generated bands also were getting big-time support from the college crowd. It wasn't long before groups and artists like the Dead Kennedys, INXS, Missing Persons, Stevie Ray Vaughan, and R.E.M. were booked and drew nice-sized crowds. The theater also aired a live video feed from Toronto for one of the Who's farewell shows.

Metal found a home at the Variety, too, with Slayer, Metallica, and others. In fact, Metallica thought enough of its Variety Theatre appearance to offer it for download on its website.

Sure, the wallpaper was peeling away in spots and it was beat up after all those years, but the vast majority were there for the performance, not the ambiance. The ceiling plaster was another story.

The date was December 2, 1984. Motorhead was booked and the audience knew what it was in for. The band roared on stage and put out a 120-decibel wall of noise. Combined with the sound of the crowd, the volume approached the level of a jet engine. Then came the unexpected. Parts of the plaster ceiling had shaken loose and were raining down on the audience. The show continued for a while, but when the band launched into its encore of "Overkill," it was time to pull the plug. The power shut down and the audience was shown the door. Clearly, the viability of the Variety Theatre as a rock venue would have to be reassessed.

There's a misconception that the Variety stopped hosting rock shows after Motorhead, but Mary Ellen Tomazic will tell you that's not true. She's a board member with Westown Community Development Corporation, which is working with the nonprofit Friends of the Historic Variety Theatre, which took ownership of the complex in 2009, to revive that venue. Quite a few shows followed in 1985 and '86, mostly punk bands sponsored by *Alternative Press* and heavily endorsed by local college radio. Among the shows in 1985 were a second round of Metallica, Venom, Exodus, Orchestral Manoeuvres in the Dark, and Suicidal Tendencies, and the Cult and Black Flag the following year. How the plaster was secured for

Neighborhood activists banded together to save the Variety Theatre (shown here in 1976), the one-time vaudeville house that almost had its walls shaken down by the band Motorhead. *(Cleveland Public Library)*

those shows is anyone's guess, but eventually the Variety Theatre stopped doing those concerts.

Over the years, Friends of the Variety and Westown CDC have campaigned to restore the theater and the building that houses it, which includes storefronts and apartment units. While progress has been slow, there has been at least one visible sign of the continuing effort to reopen the theater. Friends of the Variety and Westown CDC are working to revive that section of Lorain. The first evidence of that effort was replacing the original Variety marquee with an exact replica of the sign that opened the theater back in 1927, a sign badly damaged by a 1953 tornado. The replica's nearly 2,300 LED lights tell the public that a lot of history lies beyond the Variety's box office, and with the right funding and a little luck, there will be far more history to make.

Wilbert's Food & Music

1360 W. 9th Street, Cleveland
812 Huron Road East, Cleveland

WILBERT'S FOOD & MUSIC wasn't always easy to find. It didn't have a big, flashy sign when it opened at West 9th Street and St. Clair Avenue at the top of a hill in the Warehouse District that led down to the Flats. There was a simple wooden sign with a picture of a pepper and "Wilbert's." Same thing happened when it moved to the Caxton Building on Huron Road. You had to really look for the place, but when you found it—wow! A small place with a great kitchen and a lineup that made it well worth the search.

Michael Miller was the brains behind Wilbert's, but he didn't do it alone. When he opened the club in 1992 there were partners—and a lot of risk. Miller told the *Plain Dealer's* Fran Henry, "They say if you make it past the first three years, you're in good shape. Nobody thought I'd be here six months." But he was there all right and bought out his investors within the first five years.

Miller's family had a long history in entertainment by the time he opened Wilbert's. His great-grandfather had the George A. Miller Restaurant in the Playhouse Square area until the latter part of Prohibition; it billed itself as a place "where men serve men as men want to be served." You figure out what that means. They had a chef there named Wilbert, and George named his son, Michael's grandfather, after the guy in the big, white hat. That was his dad's name, too. Guess how the club got its name? But let's not get ahead of ourselves.

Michael Miller went to Gilmour Academy and was part of a pirate radio operation at the school until he played the uncensored version of Country Joe & the Fish's "Fish Cheer." After that ended his time at Radio Gilmour, Miller worked in the school's foodservice area. Could be a future in this! After he earned his marketing degree in 1981 from Cincinnati's Xavier University, it was off to Sanibel Island in Florida to work resorts. He was back with his parents in 1983 looking for another resort when a food and beverage management gig opened at Barney Google's lounge at the Holiday Inn Richfield. Miller started booking acts in the lounge and ballroom, including names like Albert Collins and Roy Buchanan, folks you wouldn't expect to see playing a Holiday Inn. He also started working with agencies like American Famous Talent out of Chicago. Word got around that Miller was booking names at a good penny and you got a room at the same time.

He also got an education in building lasting relationships. For example, Little Ed and the Blues Imperials weren't booked but they were looking for a room, and they slept in the ballroom.

Acts playing the Coliseum and Blossom Music Center would stop by the Richfield Holiday Inn lounge to perform. "One night Cyndi Lauper got sick after the Coliseum show with Eddie Money so they canceled the Detroit gig the next night," Miller recalls. "We ended up with Eddie Money at Barney Google's for a WMMS Night Out."

After several years at Barney Google's, Miller worked at some Cleveland clubs. A show at Bank Street at West Sixth and Lakeside Avenue, which later became Liquid, comes to mind. "One time I had a band called Goober and the Peas. I look at contract riders like wish lists. They always seem to put something in the rider just to make sure you're reading it. Goober and the Peas are an alt-country band out of Detroit, and I'm reading this rider that says they want a bale of hay! What? I told one the waitresses they wanted a bale of hay and she said, 'I'll get you one.' Where do you get a bale of hay? Turns out she worked with horses and she could get one for about five bucks. Bring it in!

"It's Friday night at the old Bank Street, and we were always packed that night. Wall to wall. The band comes in and they're head to toe in rhinestones, white suits, cowboy hats. The whole thing. People at the club look at me like, 'What did Miller book now?' I told them, 'I got you that bale of hay' and they just said thanks. It was no big deal to them. Turns out the first note they struck they threw the hay into the air and it sparkles in the stage lights! It was incredible. By the end of the night there's hay everywhere. As it turned out, the drummer was Jack White of the White Stripes. He was using the name Doc Gillis, and they all stayed at my house that night."

Time for a place to call his own.

When Wilbert's opened in 1992 it had some limitations. The stage was small, with no space in front and the bar and tables off to the side. The soundboard was in the kitchen. Who would see a show in a place like that? Turns out, plenty of people. Miller wasn't taking on the Belkins for that tier of acts. He was looking for old blues performers still working the circuit with a small but loyal audience. When it came to music Miller was a purist, and he knew how to find those acts: Koko Taylor, Pinetop Perkins, and even Johnnie Johnson, who played piano behind Chuck Berry. Up-and-coming acts, too, who he sometimes put on disc. Wilbert's Records put out CDs for acts like Blue Lunch and Wallace Coleman. "It was a calling card for the bands and it got our name out there, too," Miller says. A Blue Lunch CD was mailed out to reviewers wrapped in fake vomit—blew lunch.

There were plenty of other names, including young guitar slingers Kenny Wayne Shepherd and Jonny Lang. Buckwheat Zydeco played Cajun, Nanci Griffith performed country. Lots of blues, too, from Clarence "Gatemouth" Brown, Big Leg Emma, Albert Collins, a long list.

Anything could happen at Wilbert's. Leslie West and Mountain played some pretty bizarre stuff, including Michael Jackson's "Beat It." Despite major health issues, Leon Russell jumped on his three-wheeled scooter to zip around downtown Cleveland before his show. Katherine Isenhart, who did publicity for Wilbert's and later, Beachland, says Russell would hit all the antique stores in the Warehouse District, buy art to fill his scooter basket and head back for the show. Even blonde bombshell Anna Nicole Smith, though never booked into Wilbert's, put on quite a show on the dance floor during a visit to Cleveland. Miller says just about every artist had a story.

Debbie Harry of Blondie came to Wilbert's, backed up by the Jazz Passengers. As Miller recalls, "I had to drive her from the bar to WEWS and I thought I could take a short cut through the neighborhoods. I kept running into dead-end streets, and she asked, 'Do you know where you're going?' Believe me, I do. I just don't know this neighborhood like the back of my hand. They did a lot of jazz, but at the end people just started crying out for the Blondie hits." Isenhart, with Miller at Wilbert's since the club opened, agrees that Harry was a great performer—and a tad flirtatious with the guys.

Sometimes Miller had to weigh his options. One case was John Mayall. "He's one of those guys that gets 100 percent of my attention because he's John Mayall. He deserves it! I always made sure he was taken care of. Mayall was contracted to play the club and then the Indians got into the playoffs at the same time. I sent him half the money and said I couldn't put him up there in front of a baseball crowd that couldn't give him the respect he deserved."

Mayall played the club a number of times and always drew a big crowd. "We loved John and always made him feel really welcome," says Isenhart. "One time he stopped by and specified he wanted Texas chili; it had to be Texas chili. So I jumped in my blue truck and raced all over town until I found it. I was so proud and when I gave it to John in the club he just kind of said, 'Oh, thanks.' As I was walking out of the room I looked back to give him a smile and I saw him shoveling it into a big plastic freezer bag to eat on the road."

Some were demanding in other ways. Junior Wells was on that list.

"One of the great harp players ever," Miller said. "His roadie came up and told me, 'Mike, Junior wants four double-doubles of Tanqueray on the rocks.' Huh? Well, here's one, and when he's done with that I'll give him another. Junior wasn't happy about that. He was really mad, and the place was packed so I was helping out behind the bar. His manager came in from Chicago, walks behind the bar and says, 'I understand why you did that.' What do you mean? At that point, Wells—who was still pissed—gets on stage and yells, 'What does a guy have to do to get a drink around here!?' Next thing you know, eight drinks lined up in front of him. Everybody wanted to buy him a drink. Now he's getting overserved. What kind of show is this going to be? At the end of the night, he walked back to my office and said he had a great time, which I think his manager made him do."

Others were more cooperative, like Roger McGuinn.

"We booked Roger McGuinn, who'd been with the Byrds. Katherine Isenhart had a little blue pickup truck that I got her from an old friend of mine. We're driving down Superior Avenue and there's Roger standing by the side of the street with his wife. 'Hey Roger! I'm Mike Miller from Wilbert's. Wanna ride?' He said, 'Yeah!' and he and his wife jumped in the back of the truck. That's how cool he was."

One legend forgot to set his watch. "On New Year's Eve I had Buddy Guy. Not sure of the year, but Buddy Guy! Blue Lunch had opened up and they started at 10 (and played from) 10 to 11. Buddy was due on at 11:30 and to ring in the new year at midnight. The place is packed and everyone is having a great time. 11:30 comes and goes and I'm like, 'Where's Buddy Guy?' People are asking where he is and when does he go on. All of a sudden, it's 12 midnight and still no Buddy. I called his room and asked, 'Hey Buddy! You comin' down?' 'Yeah! I said I'd be there at 11:30.' I told him it was 10 after 12 now. He looked at his watch and said, 'Oops! I'm on Chicago time!' I hung up the phone and looked at my right-hand man Bear and said, 'I think he's on cognac time!'" But no hard feelings. "Years later I saw Buddy in his club in Chicago and I mentioned that story to him. He laughed and said, 'Yeah. I remember that gig!'"

Johnnie Johnson, who played piano on most of Chuck Berry's greatest hits, was easy to work with when he played Wilbert's. Isenhart recalls him as a real clotheshorse, always dressed to the nines.

"Johnson was happy to promote the concert, and we booked him for the morning show at WMJI. I picked him up at 6 the next day, knocked on the door, and it was obvious he just rolled out of bed. Uh-oh. How much time does he need? Johnson pulled it together and we got him there on time."

Richard Thompson was a different story: great performer, heritage act, but he didn't want to do interviews. Isenhart had to give him a firm but friendly talk detailing how much they were paying him and they needed publicity to let people know he was there. Luckily, Thompson came around.

Plenty of acts demanded perfection, like Adrian Belew. "We booked him at the club," Isenhart says, "and I loved hearing the bands do their sound check. That's where you got to interact with the bands and hear them play in a more relaxed atmosphere outside the show. Adrian Belew shows up and we shut the doors during his sound check, but it went on forever! It went through our happy hour, which didn't happen that day because he was fine-tuning his act. We had a line waiting at the door that went all the way down the hill to the Flats."

Sometimes the caliber of artist passing through the club was surprising. So were the people they chose to back them up. "John Entwistle of the Who was in the loudest band we ever had," Miller says. "He worked with a band from Nashville that were also his roadies. Six guys come in, they want a case of beer and I gave them one. Then they want another case and I pretended I didn't hear them. They were mad about that so at the end of the night they superglued the lock, and the next day my dad comes in and can't get the key in. I had to call a locksmith. But Entwistle was great, and he sat down with Jane Scott and the two were chit-chatting for hours." Interesting point: Isenhart recalls that Entwistle was actually hired by the band to use his name for that tour. Technically, that band was his boss.

Miller says artists always came through, but there were some other unexpected moments. "Peter Green used to play in Fleetwood Mac, and wrote 'Black Magic Woman,' which was a huge hit for Santana. I had my picture taken with him before he went on stage. It was back in the garage. I looked over at him and he was crying! I looked at his manager and asked what was going on? He looked over at me and said, 'Nothing. He just didn't think anyone would show tonight.' The place was packed and Green gets on stage and starts playing. It was kind of horrible. I kind of thought to myself, 'What were you thinking, Miller?! This guy has been in an insane asylum. He didn't even cash his royalty checks from the Santana song.' I thought people were going to ask for their money back. It was about the third song that the magic kicked in, and it just blew me away. It all worked out and it was a magical night. I think he was a little stunned: 'People are really here for me.' At the end of the night I asked if he would sign people's albums, and Watson [his manager] said he would, but make sure nobody touches him. I went out there and said, 'He'll be out, but do not touch him. If you do I will have to ask you to leave.' The first guy in line puts out his hand to shake it. 'Did you not hear me?'"

Autographs could be an issue.

"Some of these guys think they are too big to talk to the fans. Dude! They're the ones paying your bills!" says Miller. "Just showing a little respect goes a long way. Leon Redbone played the old place and he did a great show. At the end, he came back to my office and said, 'Hey. There's all these people that want me to sign their stuff. Can you sneak me out of here? Is there a back way?' I told him, 'Hold on a second.' I went out and told the crowd, 'I'm going to sneak Leon out through the garage in the back. Give me five minutes.' I went back and told Leon, 'I'll sneak you out through the garage!' We went out through the kitchen, I opened the garage door and there's 30 people waiting with stuff to sign. You don't pull that shit in my club! Leon never came back to play for me."

Robert Lockwood (put in the "Jr." where you like—it tended to change) was a link to blues history and a major figure in the Cleveland blues scene. He played in the old Delta blues style, learned directly from Robert Johnson, and toured with equally amazing people like Johnny Shines and Sonny Boy Williamson.

If you came to show some respect and hear what he could do, Lockwood showed his appreciation. There was a night Isenhart recalled when Lockwood was reunited with all the surviving players from radio's King Biscuit Flower Hour at the club. Miller says Lockwood also tipped his hat to another Cleveland legend, polka king Frankie Yankovic.

"That was a special night. The blues hall of famer and the polka hall of famer. Ray Davies of the Kinks came in to hear Lockwood play at the old place, and so did a couple of the guys from Tom Petty's band. It was Lockwood's 85th birthday, and Frankie Yankovic stopped in to say hello. Lockwood loved it!" Davies loved it, too. He was doing a sort of residency at Playhouse Square, and Isenhart says he made it a point to stop by Wilbert's every night he was in Cleveland. On top of that, Davies loved talking to fans.

Lockwood, meanwhile, had quite the reputation. Miller says, "Word got back to me that Taj Mahal could be difficult. I asked Lockwood if he could open for Taj Mahal and he said, 'Yeah! Absolutely.' So Taj came into the bar and set up, and he was sitting at a table that afternoon. I walked over and said, 'Taj, I want to thank you so much for playing my club.' He looked at me and said, 'Is Lockwood opening up for me, or am I opening for him?' He's opening for you. Taj shot back 'No! That's not the way it should be!' He turned out to be a totally nice guy." Totally pumped to be working with Robert Lockwood, too.

Not everyone was that cooperative: Miller tells us Dick Dale lived up to his first name. "This was right when the movie *Pulp Fiction* came out. The deal was for two grand, it was Sunday night and he told me that contract was wrong. 'It's $2,500.' I showed him the contract, but he said that was the deal. I told him, 'Know what? Let's go home.' I started shutting everything down and about 15 minutes later his girlfriend comes in crying saying, 'He said he would do it.'"

That's why people sign contracts, though some didn't like the contracts for other reasons.

Before he moved to the Caxton Building, Miller had a "disagreement" with the new owners at West 9th and St. Clair. "The owners of the building wanted me out. Different owners do it in different ways. They could put a dog in there to keep you out. I'd been there almost 10 years, new owners took over the building and in January they came in and told me 'The paperwork isn't done. As soon as it is we'll collect the rent.' On April 1 they came and gave me an eviction notice for non-payment of rent! They started pulling shit on me left and right. I hired an attorney for 10 grand and he was working on it and a few months later he said, 'Well, they don't want you there anyway.' I knew that when I gave him the 10 grand. They could have just bought me out, given me 30 grand and said, 'We want this space.' I remember calling my dad in Florida and told him they took ownership and wouldn't collect the rent. My dad said, 'I don't like this.' He had a special way or reading people. He came back and he was at the club and the owners chained the doors. He called me, I called them and said, 'I like the idea that you're trying to lock me out, but my father is in there.' Oh shit! They let him out."

Wilbert's shows continued at a place on Huron Avenue. On occasion Miller signed a diamond in the rough, and it paid off big. He paid one act $250, an act that gets a lot more for a show now: "Keith Urban came through early in his career with a band called the Ranch." John Filby saw the Ranch play Wilbert's and recognized a major star. According to Filby, "There wasn't anyone there that early, but they missed plenty. You saw this guy play and you knew that was God-given talent." After the opening set, Urban sat down next to Filby at the bar. He told Urban he worked at WMMS and promised to spread the word, prompting a big smile from Urban. The next time the Ranch played Wilbert's a lot of folks from the rock station were in attendance. Urban remembers Wilbert's fondly. Miller recalls, "We had him twice, and now every time he plays Cleveland he mentions Wilbert's."

Empire Concert Club

1012 Sumner Court, Cleveland

THE EMPIRE CONCERT CLUB was only around from 1990 to 1992, but what years! Many acts that played this tiny club could later fill arenas, including Nirvana, Pearl Jam, Warren Zevon, Stray Cats and other major headliners. When Nine Inch Nails played the Empire, Trent Reznor destroyed his keyboard onstage and then covered the audience in a huge cloud of white mist that turned out to be itching powder! Long ride home for some folks.

The Empire was on a side street of East Ninth Street near the Erie Street Cemetery. There were times when the sounds coming from the Empire could have awakened the dead.

Brothers Tony and John Ciulla booked Peabody's for a time, so they had plenty of experience when they started their own club. The place on Sumner Court was small, with room for maybe a little over 300. The Empire opened on July 3, 1990, with a show featuring Squeeze. Jason Bonham, the son of Led Zeppelin drummer John Bonham, headlined the next night.

You have to let people know you are there, and not only folks willing to pay for the big names. That December the club staged what was described as the "Grind-Grunge-Metal Festival." Bands included Terror, Phlegm, Concussion, Torment, and Screwtractor, and word got out that the club was open for business. That was the same month that someone broke into the Empire through the roof, ransacked the offices, and made off with $5,000 from the safe, a handgun, and CD player. Adding insult to injury, the thief broke a side window to escape. Life in downtown Cleveland!

A few weeks later John Mayall brought in an older audience, and the Ciullas were also auditioning local talent for the Exposure

Room, a smaller performance area that was part of the Empire. Word was getting around fast about the Empire. Soon bands like Nirvana, Rick Derringer, and Jesus Jones were packing the room, and within months of opening its doors the Empire was nominated for *Pollstar* magazine's "Nightclub Venue of the Year."

It wasn't long before the club got a face-lift. John Ciulla told the *Plain Dealer* he wanted "to make the downtown concert venue look and feel more like a big-city rock nightclub, similar to Whiskey A Go-Go in Los Angeles and CBGB's in New York City. We want to get an exciting feel, so when you come to the club to see a show the excitement builds from the second you turn the corner from E. 9th St. and see the outside of the building. Everything will symbolize rock 'n' roll. It'll be almost like a Hard Rock Cafe converted into a rock club." Mark Ciulla was also a partner, as was local business-man Ray Salupo, and they shared a vision to expand with an Italian restaurant, a couple of satellite bars, reconfiguring the walls for better stage views, and a huge mural on the exterior. They talked about mounting displays of rare rock memorabilia and of renting office space to three other tenants. The business was growing fast.

The group also wanted to highlight local talent through the weekly Empire Exposure Showcase Series. Mark Ciulla told the *PD*, "We have the proper record company base here in Cleveland. We've got the hall of fame exposure here in Cleveland. We've got several good radio stations in Cleveland. So we should be able to build this together and get these people the exposure they need." Sixty bands showed up for the first audition, some with a lot more experience than others, and the Ciulla team said it would help guide any promising talent. Word got around quick and another 40 bands knocked on the door within days of the first tryouts.

Not all the action was on stage. Ric Bennett, aka Rocco, the Rock Dog, from WMMS, set up a tent on the roof of the building for a station promotion that would fill a semi-trailer in the parking lot with food. He said he wouldn't come down until the truck was full, and thankfully, the power of the Buzzard brought plenty of people out before winter blew in. Rocco had his feet on the ground in just five days.

The Empire had issues with occupancy. It topped out at 730 if everyone stood for the show, which limited the magnitude of acts the club could book. The management looked for bigger rooms to book up to 2,000, but other promoters were looking for those same places. There were still plenty of acts that played a venue that size. The Ramones filled the Empire and played 30 songs in 80 minutes, but many of the acts just got too big to play that stage. That left up-and-comers like Psychefunkapus out of San Francisco, which drew wide praise for its first album but was pretty much unknown on the east coast, drawing a meager crowd to the Empire. The numbers were dropping. Something had to give, which it did on a Saturday night in April 1992.

Buddy Guy packed the club, and who should stop by that night but the fire marshal. He said the club was at least 150 over the limit and about a half-hour into Guy's set he stopped the concert. People were pissed, and it got real tense very quickly. Guy sat in the dressing room and maybe an hour later the show resumed after 200 people took a full refund. This wasn't over, however. The fire marshal said there were only two exits, and one was partially blocked by a couple of dumpsters and some parked cars. Plus, let's face it. In an emergency, patrons weren't going to line up in an orderly manner and file out one by one. The Ciullas said the real danger arose when the show was called. It could have been a mob scene! Still, here's a rule of thumb. You battle the city, the city usually wins, and the Empire found that out the hard way.

Citing alleged complaints about overcrowding, the fire department got together with the Cleveland Building and Housing Division and told the Ciullas the club's maximum standing room was now officially 317 people. How do you attract top talent with a sell-out crowd of 317?! Now what?

Talks continued with the city that indicated that a redesign of the Empire floor plan could expand occupancy to 500. One thing for certain: The fire marshal was going to keep a close eye on the place, so bigger shows needed a bigger venue. Maybe they could book the Agora or the Phantasy, but the Empire would be held to its limit. The other shoe dropped that summer.

Just before the July 4 weekend, the Ciullas got word that the city didn't like the redesign plans and occupancy would top out at 317. You can't book bigger acts at that capacity so the Ciullas had a couple of options: book smaller acts and basically become a glorified beer joint or shut the doors. There were plenty of watering holes in downtown Cleveland, especially in the Flats, so the Ciullias decided to shut down. There were still some shows coming up, with Bob Mould from Husker Du, Helmet, and Bad Religion, and some acts like Tori Amos were transferred to other clubs.

The Empire officially closed on July 22. When it went toe-to-toe with the city, the Empire couldn't strike back. It struck out.

Amusement Parks

Chippewa Lake Park, Euclid Beach Park,
Geauga Lake Park

IN THE EARLY DAYS of amusement parks, ballroom events drew people and the rides were added as an afterthought. Many parks were social centers, with music seven days a week. But rock and roll brought a whole new dynamic to amusement park shows. When they began, you had a chance to see future inductees to the Rock and Roll Hall of Fame driving up and even unloading their own equipment.

Chippewa Lake Park in Medina County saw its share. New York's Young Rascals were radio staples when they played Chippewa Lake back in the mid-'60s. There was a WIXY Appreciation Day show in May 1966 with the Vogues, the GTOs, Beau Brummels and . . . hold on to your hat . . . Vic Dana! The rock and roll umbrella covered a lot of Top 40 acts back then.

There was also the Ohio Teen Fair, a weekend series of shows at the park in August 1966 featuring some pretty impressive names. There were three shows a day including a matinee at 3 p.m., with Gary Lewis and the Playboys kicking it off on a Thursday. Lewis had a long list of hits, but the interesting act at this show was the opener, Napoleon XIV. He had a hit with the novelty song, "They're Coming to Take Me Away, Ha-Haaa!" (It was later pulled from many radio playlists for mocking mental illness.) There was another good show on Friday with Cleveland's own Outsiders opening for Mitch Ryder and the Detroit Wheels, and Saturday showcased the McCoys, with Harvey Russell and the Rogues as the opener. Russell was an Akron cop who moonlighted as a singer and had a hit with "Shake Sherry." It all wrapped up on Sunday with shows by the Shangri-Las and Terry Knight and the Pack before it eventually morphed into Grand Funk Railroad.

There were always crowds at amusement parks because Northeast Ohio hung on to every bit of summer that it could, but radio could inflate the numbers at the gate to near-Woodstock proportions. Here are some examples:

Euclid Beach had a national reputation. It welcomed stars of radio back in the 1930s and '40s, John F. Kennedy drew record crowds in an appearance just weeks before the 1960 presidential election, and an episode of TV's *Route 66* titled "Two on the House" featured the park. The Humphrey family owned Euclid Beach and ran a tight ship. It was a family park, and it never sold beer. In fact, the family reserved the right to deny entry to anyone who looked like they had had a few before they arrived at the park. In the early '60s they looked for family attractions, and in August 1964 they booked a California band that was getting lots of attention: the Beach Boys.

Plenty of acts had played Euclid Beach, including Jan and Dean, but the Beach Boys were in a class all by themselves. They were led by songwriter Brian Wilson, the teenager labeled as a pop music genius and praised by the Beatles and other British Invasion groups fighting for Top 40 space. The band made a quick stop in the Midwest for a couple of shows in August 1964 at Euclid Beach and an appearance down the road at Pittsburgh's Syria Mosque. You wanted clean-cut? These were the days when the band even dressed up for appearances, wearing their matching signature Pendleton shirts and hair that barely touched their ears.

The show was sponsored by Cleveland's KYW and jocks including Jay Lawrence, Jerry G. Bishop and the rest of the staff welcomed fans to the park's old wooden ballroom. The Beach Boys drew a respectable crowd and played their hits.

At that time, Euclid Beach had a long-standing reputation as being more "friendly" to white patrons. It tended to book acts for a specific audience. It also had a lot of competition, and as early as 1966 was looking to move some operations to land the Hum-

Neil Diamond's star was just beginning to rise and the era of huge rock festivals was yet to come when the WIXY Appreciation Day drew a crowd estimated at more than 100,000 to Geauga Lake Park. *(George Shuba)*

phrey family owned in Streetsboro Township. Oddly enough, that was right around the corner from Geauga Lake Amusement Park, which also was looking to attract the rock audience.

Geauga Lake had a long history of attracting crowds to its ballroom shows. Big bands and dance shows were a huge draw, and some were even broadcast live over local radio. But that was before rock and roll radio, and stations like WHK and KYW had a lot of influence. They staged some very popular shows at Geauga Lake, but WIXY 1260 took it to a whole new level.

WIXY first took to the air in late 1965. It was a small station with a very limited broadcast signal, but it had a big sound and even bigger promotion ideas. The DJs' voices jumped out of your speakers and it seemed something exciting was going on every time you switched on the station. The folks at WIXY also knew you had to back up what you promoted. The station presented some shows at Chippewa Lake, but Geauga Lake had more room and was more accessible. In July 1967, the station held its first WIXY Appreciation Day at Geauga Lake, taking a big risk on both date and location.

The show was scheduled for a Tuesday at a park in Portage County that the WIXY signal barely reached. Then again, the station knew it would draw from across Northeast Ohio—but no one anticipated just how big a draw. On the day of the show, thousands of cars jammed State Route 43 heading to the park long before it opened. Many started out early because there was a daylong schedule of events leading up to showtime including a miniature golf derby against the WIXY jocks, a record hop for the first 1,000 arrivals, and, of course, all the rides. One problem: Many of the disc jockeys and the artists were in that same traffic jam going nowhere fast.

It was a pretty impressive list of acts, too. The Fifth Dimension had a hit with "Up, Up and Away" and were getting a lot of TV time. Tommy Boyce and Bobby Hart had written hits for the Monkees and other groups and were now on the road themselves. Tommy Roe had a string of hits, and Every Mother's Son was topping the charts with "Come On Down To My Boat." There was a newcomer, too, that no one recognized. In fact, when the acts finally took the stage that evening the young songwriter spent most of his time sitting by a tree enjoying the show. Finally, WIXY's Larry Morrow took the mic and called him to the stage. "Hey everybody! A young guy with a bright future! Let's give a big hand for—Neil Diamond!"

There were other appreciation days and special events, but the crowning achievement may have been the Appreciation Day on August 2, 1968, when WIXY was at its peak. It had driven WHK and WKYC (the former KYW) to other formats and FM radio was still a novelty. It was a Thursday in the final month of summer vacation. The station announced a lineup with eight acts including Gene Pitney, the GTOs, the New Colony Six, the 1910 Fruitgum Company, the Box Tops, Jay and the Techniques, the Peppermint Trolley Company and the Amboy Dukes featuring (there's that name again), Ted Nugent. This was an indication of what Top 40 radio was like, a lineup covering everything form hard rock to bubblegum, all in regular rotation on WIXY.

This was also a goldmine of promotional opportunities for the station. Geauga Lake officials wanted a big show at the gate, but not headaches of traffic tie-ups. Many families would just be there for the rides, too, so the WIXY call letters would get noticed a lot. Here was the deal: WIXY would pick up the tab for free admission to the park starting at 2 p.m., along with free parking and half-price rides. There would be plenty of free prizes, too, ranging from milk shakes and makeup kits to transistor radios, but you had to sign up to volunteer for WIXY's march to fight leukemia. There would be hundreds of free tickets for Police Athletic League and League Park Center kids. So how would the station fight traffic with all that going on? How about busing in the crowds?

WIXY contracted with the Cleveland Transit System for radio-equipped buses to pick up concertgoers from Parmatown, Southgate, and Richmond Mall shopping centers and in downtown Cleveland at the mall near the Federal Building. Buses left every 15 to 30 minutes at 50 cents a head, returning after the show. All this free stuff, plus buses. How many people were they expecting?

The numbers turned out like you wouldn't believe. WIXY's Larry Morrow took the mic to announce, "There's never been this many people anywhere!" The Beatles drew 44,000 to Shea Stadium and 25,000 to Candlestick Park on their 1966 tour. In 1967, the Monterey Pop Festival could fit 8,500 for its top performers.

The WIXY Appreciation Day show may well have been the largest concert before Woodstock the very next year. Crowd estimates topped 120,000. It was shoulder-to-shoulder most of the day, with only an occasional hitch, like a stalled car here and there; Jay and the Techniques' equipment truck was in an accident on the turnpike. The band still did its show, borrowing the GTOs' gear. Were they all there because of WIXY? Probably not, but they all heard the music and had a great story to tell when they left the park that day.

Bruce Springsteen wrote, "the amusement park rises bold and stark," but these Cleveland-area venues eventually went cold and dark. Euclid Beach closed in September 1969 and Chippewa Lake ended its 100-year history in 1978. Geauga Lake hung on until 2007, its nearby water park a while longer. The abandoned buildings and roller coasters cast a long shadow, conjuring a time when thousands would gather like great tribes to cheer on their heroes. Northeast Ohio had plenty of heroes, with plenty of places to see them.

Afterword

FOLKS USED TO SAY "rock and roll will never die," but you have to wonder what rock and roll is these days. When Pete Townshend was inducted into the Rock and Roll Hall of Fame in 1990, he discussed new music by saying "It's not up to us to understand it. It's not even up to us to buy it. We just have to get the fuck out of the way!" You're right, Pete. Change is inevitable and the only constant, and we have to accept it. Rock and roll means a lot of different things and we define it according to the way it affects us. Much of the way we define it comes from experiencing it live and remembering the importance of the event and the people we shared it with. That could be in a smoky basement bar, an elegant nightclub, a massive stadium or even a cow field. The best memories may come from the venues where you live, that common ground that makes you think, "I'm from Northeast Ohio and it happened right here."

Those who saw shows at the Mirror Bar, Dove Lounge, the Hippodrome, or any of the early sites probably wouldn't recognize today's pop charts as rock and roll. But how many people who see Lady Gaga at Quicken Loans Arena can relate to those early pioneers in a similar way? What unites us is the related experience, that connection with the artist that makes us a part of the music we choose to listen to. We can become one with the music in any form that rock and roll chooses to take.

What was your favorite concert? Why and where? Was it a major act or some unknown artist? Robert Jr. Lockwood once said he was sure that Robert Johnson played Ohio because they were on the same circuit. They didn't play concert halls. It could have been in a small club or living room or even a barn or garage where they passed the hat. Johnson's music is still played in the biggest venues and heard by millions. For the precious few who heard him pick out those first blues numbers, it was that shared experience that helped keep his legend alive, along with some very crude but profoundly insightful recordings.

Rock and roll venues have been referred to as the "electric church." Although we shouldn't revive that John Lennon controversy as to which is more important, we should see the similarities in a community finding inspiration through an emotional bond. There are giant ornate cathedrals and massive performance centers, and there are storefront churches that can be likened to small stages in a club or bar. People gather for the same reason: the bond that comes from connecting with the person sharing a message. The Cleveland area has shown it has something for everyone's needs.

Does rock and roll even exist anymore, or has it become so splintered by programmers and consultants and the ways it's marketed that it's evolved into some other type of art form? Maybe we can just call it popular music. With respect to fans of many new artists, we think you can agree that rock and roll is a lifestyle and part of that lifestyle is seeing and growing with the musicians in raw live performances. Is rock and roll becoming a memory? Let's keep our memories alive. A popular T-shirt and bumper sticker you see now and then states, "I'm old, but I saw all the cool bands!" If you were lucky, you got to see them in one of Cleveland's rock and roll venues.

Acknowledgments

SPECIAL THANKS TO Kitty Andrus, Cliff Baechle, Tom Baechle, Bob Brandt, Ray Carr, D.X. Ferris, Brad Funk, Eric Funk, Rick Funk, David Gray, Bianca Kontra, Angelina Leas, John Luttermoser, Buddy Maver, Brian Meggett, Cate Misciagna, Cole Misciagna, Cora Misciagna, Jenny Misciagna, Tony Misciagna, Vern Morrison, Joan Olszewski, Larry Petit, Theresa Phillips, Marion Pigon, Scott Shepherd, Steve Traina, Cindi Verbulen, Carlo Wolff.

We also express sincere gratitude to the late Linas Johansonas for his passionate support in promoting the Northeast Ohio music scene. Esame garbę skambinti tau mūsų draugu. Jūsų atmintis gyvens amžinai.

And finally, our sincere thanks to every librarian, photographer, and newspaper writer who documented these important events. You were eyewitnesses to an important part of Northeast Ohio history, and we appreciate your diligence. You made our job so much easier.

We also encourage you to visit the websites of the artists who helped us bring you the history outlined in this book including:

George Shuba: Shuba & Associates Photography, 4347 Pearl Rd, Cleveland, OH 44109

Janet Macoska: www.janetmacoskaphotography.com

Derek Hess: www.derekhess.com

Lew Allen: www.rockpaperphoto.com

Bibliography

Unattributed Articles

"$10,000 Suit Tells Rift at Gleason's." *Call & Post.* December 8, 1951.

"61.9% Prefer Coliseum Here." *Plain Dealer.* April 11, 1973.

"A Rock for the Stones." *Plain Dealer.* November 30, 1981.

"About the Stars." *Call & Post.* July 20, 1963.

"About the Stars." *Call & Post.* October 3, 1964.

"Adult Movie Gets Lakewood Ouster." *Plain Dealer.* April 25, 1972.

"Ahmad Jamal, Bobby Bland Leo's Casino Attractions." *Call & Post.* May 8, 1965.

"Alan Freed to Emcee Rhythm and Blues Show." *Call & Post.* August 7, 1954.

"Arena Management Steers Moondog Dance Promotion." *Call & Post.* May 10, 1952.

"Aretha Coming Into Leo's Casino Thurs." *Call & Post.* December 11, 1965.

"At Gleason's for Pauletta: Ex-Barmaid, Ill, Gets Benefit Party Sunday." *Call & Post.* November 9, 1957.

"At Leo's Casino This Week, Next Week." *Call & Post.* November 5, 1966.

"B.B. King at Leo's Casino." *Call & Post.* October 2, 1965.

"B.B. King at Leo's Casino." *Call & Post.* July 3, 1966.

"B.B. King's Big Show Packing Leo's Casino." *Call & Post.* August 1, 1964.

"Big Joe Turner 'Blues Boss' Into Gleason's April 3." *Call & Post.* March 28, 1959.

"Big Maybelle into Gleason's." *Call & Post.* April 2, 1960.

"Blues Accordion Man Swings into Gleason's With Band Next Week." *Call & Post.* November 2, 1957.

"Candy Johnson to Gleason's Musical Bar on Thanksgiving." *Call & Post.* November 12, 1949.

"Charge 14,000 Sale for 'Moondog Ball'." *Plain Dealer.* March 23, 1952.

"Cleveland Rock Legends." *Plain Dealer.* October 15, 2000.

Cleveland Rocks Past / Present / Future. [Larry Bruner notes for interview by S. Traina]. (2012, November 3). In *Steve's Folk.* Cleveland, OH: WCSB-FM.

"Club Trinidad Joins parade: Sets Up Talent Time with Eckstine as M.C.." *Call & Post.* May 14, 1955.

"Coming attractions in the Flats." *Cleveland Press.* January 9, 1970.

"Concerts live despite World Series demise." *Plain Dealer.* August 7, 1979.

"Congo First, Now Gleason's Present Talent Night Shows." *Call & Post.* February 26, 1955.

"Cool jazz on draught at Smiling Dog Saloon." *Plain Dealer.* October 13, 1972.

"Cootie and Cleanhead Hit High at Gleason's." *Call & Post.* August 14, 1954.

"Dizzy Gillespie is Coming to Gleason's." *Call & Post.* April 11, 1953.

"Dionne Warwick At Leo's." *Call & Post.* April 1, 1967.

"Famed Isley Brothers Coming To Gleason's." *Call & Post.* October 27, 1962.

"Fashion Show At Leo's Casino March 30 Looms As Largest Of The Spring Season." *Call & Post.* March 22, 1969.

"Fats Domino Opens at Gleason's Monday." *Call & Post.* November 27, 1954.

"Feedback." *Plain Dealer.* October 15, 1976.

"Fleetwood Mac concertgoers are rob victims." *Cleveland Press.* August 28, 1978.

"Four Tops At Leo's Through July Fourth." *Call & Post.* July 2, 1966.

"Gladys Knight & Pips Open at Leo's Sept. 11." *Call & Post.* September 6, 1969.

"Gleason's Loses $35." *Call & Post.* August 7, 1954.

"Gleason's Musical Bar Sparkles As Bass Ashford Offers Jump Sensation." *Call & Post.* July 29, 1950.

"Harrison has second show." *Plain Dealer.* November 1, 1974.

"Jackie Brenston Steals Limelight At Moondog Ball." *Call & Post.* May 24, 1952.

"Jackie Wilson Into Gleason's." *Call & Post.* September 27, 1958.

"J. Thompson's Treats Customers To Night Out At Leo's Casino." *Call & Post.*

"'King of Moondogs' To Leave Cleveland." *Call & Post.* July 17, 1954.

"Leo's Casino," *Cleveland Historical*, accessed March 26, 2017, https://cleveland-historical.org/items/show/5.

"Leo's Casino May Reopen." *Call & Post.* May 5, 1983.

"Leo's Casino Open Again." *Call & Post.* October 3, 1970.

"Leo's Casino Seeking to Raise $5000 for Slain Cabbie's Family." *Call & Post.* October 31, 1964

"Leo's Is Open Again: Unveil Newly Decorated Front; Spur Name Contest." *Call & Post.*

"Leo's Jumps with Go-Go Girls In Lounge, 'Blue Eyed Soul Brother' In Big Casino." *Call & Post.* June 22, 1968.

"Leo's Opening Really Grand." *Call & Post.* July 24, 1954.

"Leo's Remodeling; To Have Policy Of 52 Shows A Year." *Call & Post.* September 24, 1966.

"Leo's Serves No Alcohol This Week: Staple Singers Head Gospel Singing Spectacle at Casino." *Call & Post.* August 5, 1967.

"Lights Go On Again At Leo's For Otis Redding's Revue Sat., Dec. 9." *Call & Post.* December 2, 1967.

"Little Esther Coming To Leo's Casino." *Call & Post.* July 9, 1966.

"Little Man, Big Horn: Chamblee's Sax At Musical Bar." *Call & Post.* April 26, 1952.

"LSD Charges Denied by 4 Nabbed as Drug Suspects." *Cleveland Press.* May 14, 1968.

"Martha & Vandellas, Richard Pryor Makes Leo's Casino Tops This Week." *Call & Post.* March 23, 1968.

"Marvin Gaye At Leo's." *Call & Post.* January 11, 1964.

"Marvin Gaye Scores Big At Leo's Casino." *Call & Post.* July 11, 1964.

"Mary Wells at Leo's." *Call & Post.* November 13, 1965.

"'Moon-Dog Robbery' Defendants are Free." *Call & Post.* June 13, 1953.

"Moondog Ball Is Halted as 6,000 Crash Arena Gate." *Plain Dealer.* March 22, 1952.

"'Moondog' Brinnon of WJW to Emcee Circle's Battle of the Song." *Call & Post.* October 30, 1954.

"Moondog Madness." *Call & Post.* March 29, 1952.

"Moondog May Time Ball Gets Started Quietly at Arena." *Plain Dealer.* May 18, 1952.

"Moondog May Time Ball Threatens Arena Record." *Call & Post.* May 7, 1952.

"Moondog Promoter Weeps in His Beer." *Call & Post.* March 29, 1952.

""Moondoggers Ball" Has Two Shows Today." *Plain Dealer.* May 18, 1952.

"Muddy Waters Comes to Gleason's Monday." *Call & Post.* March 9, 1957.

"Ojays Head Pre-Christmas Production At Leo's Casino." *Call & Post.* December 23, 1967.

"Only 2000 See Arena Show: Mayor, Police Caused Flop, Says, 'Crazy Man'." *Call & Post.* February 12, 1955.

"Picker's illness silences concert." *Plain Dealer.* August 5, 1978.

"Promoter Belkin kills 2nd Rock World Series." *Plain Dealer.* August 3, 1979.

"Public Hall Ban Ousts Monkees." *Plain Dealer.* April 6, 1967.

"Quad Hall to House Newest Night Club." *Plain Dealer.* September 8, 1963.

"Ray Charles On The Way: "It Should've Been Me" Singer Into Gleason's." *Call & Post.* July 31, 1954.

"Ray Charles Will 'Drown in Tears' for Gleason's Musical Bar Dancers." *Call & Post.* November 3, 1956.

"Rock Concert goers litter downtown." *Cleveland Press.* June 27, 1977.

"Roots of Black Entertainment: Yesterday and Today." *Call & Post.* June 14, 1990.

"Rhythm Hits Leo's Casino." *Call & Post.* April 18, 1964.

"Schoolhouse Rock." *Cleveland Magazine.* March 27, 2007.

"Smokey & The Miracles at Leo's." *Call & Post.* June 17, 1967.

"Solomon Burke, Band, Revue, Now at Leo's." *Call & Post.* August 28, 1965.

"Soul and Sound: The Supremes at Leo's." *Call & Post.* July 16, 1966.

"Sound Off . . . " *Plain Dealer.* October 25, 1972.

"Steer Roast Called Off." *Call & Post.* October 2, 1965.

"Step-N-Fetchit At Leo's Casino." *Call & Post.* January 18, 1964.

"Stones hope to return in 1983." *Plain Dealer.* November 20, 1981.

"Stevie Wonder Will Play Sunday Matinee At Leo's." *Call & Post.* July 15, 1967.

"Sues Promoters of Moondog Ball." *Call & Post.* April 19, 1952.

"Temptations Head Big Show At Leo's Casino." *Call & Post.* August 14, 1965.

"The Swallows: Freed's Moonlight Moondoggers To Play Crystal Beach, Akron, Girard." *Call & Post.* June 21, 1952.

"Thieves open safe, take $5000 at club." *Plain Dealer.* December 27, 1991.

"The Winner!" *Plain Dealer.* November 2, 1973.

"Tiny on Way: No Door Charges at Gleason's For Grimes." *Call & Post.* January 30, 1954.

Smoky, Sweaty, Rowdy & Loud

"Today's Youngsters: Teen-Agers or Moon-Doggers?" *Call & Post*. May 3, 1952.

"Top Attractions Coming To Leo's." *Call & Post*. August 10, 1978.

"Trotters and Indians Help Fill Niteries." *Call & Post*. April 18, 1953.

"Willio and Phillio: Humor and harmony." *Plain Dealer*. March 17, 1978.

Bylined Articles

Adonees Sarrouh, "Gleason's Musical Bar," *Cleveland Historical*, accessed March 12, 2017, <https://clevelandhistorical.org/items/show/634March 28>.

Albrecht, Brian. "Musicians arrested at awards show." *Plain Dealer*. February 26, 2005.

Anable, Anna. "'Hot" Times Ahead." *Plain Dealer*. April 8, 1971.

Barmana, George. "Champagne flows at Coliseum. Mileti, Sinatra share spotlight." *Plain Dealer*. October 27, 1974.

Beard, David. "Fans, vans flock to see final fling of Who for U.S." *Plain Dealer*. December 14, 1982.

Beard, David & Jane Scott. "Even grandmas love the Stones." *Plain Dealer*. November 18, 1981.

Bellamy, Peter. "New showplace to open in June." *Plain Dealer*. February 5, 1974.

Bellamy, Peter. "There's no end in sight for Musicarnival arena." *Plain Dealer*. July 28, 1974.

Bornino, Bruno. "88,000 rock fans win Modell's praise." *Cleveland Press*. September 2, 1974.

Bornino, Bruno. "Elvis Overwhelms 22,000 in the Coliseum." *Cleveland Press*. July 11, 1975.

Bornino, Bruno. "Fans 'get religion' at Stadium concert." *Cleveland Press*. August 28, 1978.

Bornino, Bruno. "Stadium rocks inside and out." *Cleveland Press*. June 27, 1977.

Bryant, Shirlee. "East Hi-Lites." *Call & Post*. March 22, 1952.

Bryant, Shirlee. "East Hi-Lites." *Call & Post*. May 10, 1952.

Cheeks, Dwayne. "Area is feeling impact of reggae." *Plain Dealer*. July 29, 1983.

DeMarco, Laura. "Inside look: Cleveland's historic Variety Theatre coming back to life." *Plain Dealer*. August 7, 2015.

Diadiun, Ted. "Euclid Beach Ballroom, Leo's Casino and La Cave for intimate (and cheap) concerts: Cleveland Remembers." *Plain Dealer*. August 25, 2011.

Eyman, Scott. "LoConti: A baron in the kingdom of nightspots with a canny eye for success." *Plain Dealer Sunday Magazine*. June 26, 1977.

Feran, Tom. "The Mintz behind rock 'n' roll myth." *Plain Dealer*. March 22, 2002.

Ferris, D.X. "Odeon Out." *Scene*. February 22, 2006.

Forte, Roland. "Edwin Hawkins Singers mix pop, gospel." *Plain Dealer*. April 11, 1975.

Forte, Roland. "Odetta and 'baby' bring audiences right into her 'home'." *Plain Dealer*. February 1, 1974.

Fuster, John. "About the Stars." *Call & Post*. May 15, 1958.

Fuster, John. "About the Stars." *Call & Post.* September 8, 1956.

Fuster, John. "About the Stars." *Call & Post.* September 19, 1959.

Fuster, John. "Barmaids And Waitresses Serve Beggars And Kings." *Call & Post.* September 22, 1951.

Gambol, Lisa. "Punk band inspires gentler pit action." *Plain Dealer.* December 5, 1994.

Gerdel, Thomas. "Coliseum seeks image beyond world of sports." *Plain Dealer.* August 6, 1978.

Heaton, Michael. "Famed hotel owner Jim Swingos takes a long look back on the glory days." *Plain Dealer.* November 1, 2013.

Heaton, Michael. "Minister goes out on ellipse . . . to bring you the who's, where's, whyfores of the newest entry in the local club scene." *Plain Dealer.* March 10, 2000.

Heaton, Michael. "Variety spices up Cleveland nightlife." *Plain Dealer.* June 24, 1988.

Henry, Fran. "Michael Miller." *Plain Dealer.* December 18, 1996.

Hitchcock, Craig & Susan Chace. "Rock Violence is Probed." *Cleveland Press.* July 30, 1979.

Holmes, Robert J. "Cleveland Area LSD Ring Smashed." *Plain Dealer.* May 14, 1968.

Jackson, John A. Big Beat Heat: Alan Freed And the Early Years of Rock & Roll. Schirmer Trade Books; New York, NY.

Jenkins, Jr., Willard. "Peabody's Café stresses diversity in music." *Plain Dealer.* June 2, 1978.

Kay, Leslie. "The Beatles are gone but Paul is back." *Plain Dealer.* May 11, 1976.

Kelly, Michael. "1966 Last Year for Euclid Beach?" *Plain Dealer.* August 26, 1965.

Kinney, Brian. "Some fans got off on music, others high on marijuana." *Cleveland Press.* September 2, 1979.

Kisner, Kathy. "The Original Datebook Co." *Plain Dealer.* September 25, 1987.

Lee, Howard. "Choker Campbell's Music Keeps Up Reputation of Gleason's Musical Bar." *Call & Post.* February 5, 1949.

Lenhart Jr., Harry A. "Kaye, Gleason Due for Fairview Party." *Plain Dealer.* November 19, 1963.

Lifton, Dave. "The Time Bruce Springsteen Got Hit in the Face With a Lit Firecracker." http://ultimateclassicrock.com/bruce-springsteen-firecracker-show/ December 31, 2014.

Long, John S. "It's the end of the line for Dick's Last Resort." *Plain Dealer.* September 3, 2003.

McLaughlin, Mary. "Forecast of Flats Fun." *Plain Dealer.* April 22, 1971.

Miller, Marilyn, James Calder, and Erin Bell, "Euclid Tavern," *Cleveland Historical,* accessed May 19, 2017, https://clevelandhistorical.org/items/show

Minke, Dick. "Old Folks." *Live in Cleveland.* Vol. 3, No. 5. October 3, 1993.

Minke, Dick. "Old Folks." *Live in Cleveland.* Vol. 3, No. 6. November 27, 1993

Mona, Breanna. "When the Beatles Came to Town." *Northeast Ohio Boomer & Beyond.* July / August 2016.

Norman, Michael. "Band wraps empire in its funk 'n' roll." *Plain Dealer*. February 7, 1992.

Norman, Michael. "Belkin wins battle of the bookings." *Plain Dealer*. January 7, 1996.

Norman, Michael. "Coffee Break Concert gets shot of Metallica." *Plain Dealer*. February 20, 1997.

Norman, Michael. "Down and dirty sounds emerge from depths of Slash's snakepit." *Plain Dealer*. April 26, 1995.

Norman, Michael. "Empire closing doors this month." *Plain Dealer*. July 11, 1992.

Norman, Michael. "Fans at Odeon get serious about moshing to familiar tunes." *Plain Dealer*. November 21, 1996.

Norman, Michael. "Last Time a sellout, Rod Stewart's show returns." *Plain Dealer*. December 13, 1999.

Norman, Michael. "Nancy Sinatra sets boots on comeback trail." *Plain Dealer*. May 16, 1995.

Norman, Michael. "Nine Inch Nails surprises with club gig." *Plain Dealer*. December 30, 1994.

Norman, Michael. "Noted bluesman electrifying in Odeon concert." *Plain Dealer*. February 23, 1995.

Norman, Michael. "Peabody's DownUnder, flagship of the Flats and one of the best concert clubs: Cleveland Remembers." *Plain Dealer*. May 23, 2011.

Norman, Michael. "Rock-club owner is doing a little empire building." *Plain Dealer*. January 25, 1992.

Norman, Michael. "Show-stopping fire inspectors have club owners singing blues." *Plain Dealer*. April 20, 1992.

Norman, Michael. "The Artist no Prince to after-show partygoers." *Plain Dealer*. May 20, 1997.

Norman, Michael. "Tight seating is squeezing Empire Club." *Plain Dealer*. June 6, 1992.

O'Connor, Clint. "How safe are city's nightclubs? Fire crews patrol to avert repeat of recent tragedies." *Plain Dealer*. April 27, 2003.

Pantsios, Anastasia. "More and more clubs are hot after bands playing originals." *Plain Dealer*. March 11, 1983.

Pantsios, Anastasia. "Multi-screen video on the rise as entertainment in nightspots." *Plain Dealer*. April 20, 1984.

Pantsios, Anastasia. "New out-of-town acts get break." *Plain Dealer*. April 22, 1983.

Pantsios, Anastasia. "Punk Rockers." *Plain Dealer*. May 4, 1977.

Pantsios, Anastasia. "Trend Setters." *Plain Dealer*. June 12, 1980.

Pantsios, Anastasia. "Wilbert's Part Deux Mike Miller resurrects his club at a new downtown site, with the same fun and flair." *Plain Dealer*. September 12, 2003.

Perkins, Olivera. "Cleveland groups aim to revive 'Main Street'. Experts shape formula to draw business." *Plain Dealer*. March 10, 2001.

Petkovic, John. "Arthur Lee and Love are roaring back, ready to rock." *Plain Dealer*. August 2, 2002.

Petkovic, John. "A two-night birthday bash at the Beachland Ballroom." *Plain Dealer*. February 24, 2002.

Petkovic, John. "Legendary Cleveland Agora club owner Hank LoConti has died, leaves behind world-renowned legacy." *Plain Dealer*. July 9, 2014.

Petkovic, John. "Storied Cleveland Flats music club The Odeon to reopen." *Plain Dealer*. March 16, 2015.

Petkovic, John. "Storied Phantasy Entertainment Complex in Lakewood up for sale." *Plain Dealer*. July 10, 2015.

Petkovic, John. "Swingos hotel: Where rockers raged and legends were made in the 1970s." *Plain Dealer*. October 15, 2000.

Petkovic, John. "The Hives are itching to get to the Beachland Ballroom." *Plain Dealer*. June 2, 2002.

Petkovic, John. "Troubadour visits blues blowout." *Plain Dealer*. April 8, 1999.

Pinckard, Cliff. "James Swingos, owner of former Cleveland hot spot Swingos Celebrity Inn, dies at age 73." *Plain Dealer*. August 12, 2015.

Pullen, Glenn C. "Capt. Bligh's 'Bounty' is anchored." Plain Dealer. March 7, 1969.

Pullen, Glenn C. "Frolic at Americana Is an Uneasy Blend." *Plain Dealer*. November 30, 1963.

Puller, Glenn C. "Gillespie's Weirdies Please Addicts Only." *Plain Dealer*. November 22, 1963.

Pullen, Glenn C. "Joe Williams Won't Stop Moaning Blues." *Plain Dealer*. November 8, 1963.

Pullen, Glenn C. "Saints to go marching in, out, down, up Flats streets." *Plain Dealer*. September 25, 1970.

Richardson, Marty. "Today's Youngsters: Teen-Agers or Moon-Doggers?" *Call & Post*. April 19, 1952.

Richardson, Marty. "Today's Youngsters: Teen-Agers or Moon-Doggers?" *Call & Post*. April 26, 1952.

Richmond, John. "Crowd gets blues from tardy star." *Plain Dealer*. September 26, 1985.

Robertson, Don. "Beatles Gone; Malady Lingers." *Plain Dealer*. September 17, 1964.

Robertson, Don. "Screaming Beatle Fans Stop Show for 10 Minutes." *Plain Dealer*. September 16, 1964.

Salisbury, Wilma. "The Flats Scene." *Plain Dealer*. April 8, 1977.

Sangiacomo, Michael. "Vocals hallmark of sisters' performance." *Plain Dealer*. June 19, 1992.

Schneider, Russell. "Schneider Around." *Plain Dealer*. February 16, 1975.

Scott, Jane. "2 Live Crew set to rap here." *Plain Dealer*. August 31, 1990.

Scott, Jane. "A flight of Phantasy." *Plain Dealer*. July 9. 1976.

Scott, Jane. "A former Wolf in the Palace." *Plain Dealer*. April 21, 1989.

Scott, Jane. "Aussies head for Front Row." *Plain Dealer*. April 24, 1987.

Scott, Jane. "B-52s scheduled for landing." *Plain Dealer*. October 27, 1989.

Scott, Jane. "Bag rocking with country twang." *Plain Dealer*. February 2, 1990.

Scott, Jane. "Bands' sounds varied, but all groups rock with power." *Plain Dealer*. November 10, 1997.

Scott, Jane. "Belkin Productions buys the Odeon in the Flats." *Plain Dealer*. March 13, 1996.

Scott, Jane. "Billy Joel makes it 4-timer." *Plain Dealer*. March 30, 1990.

Scott, Jane. "Bob Seger returns Feb. 19." *Plain Dealer*. January 30, 1987.

Scott, Jane. "Book of Love back." *Plain Dealer*. March 6, 1987.

Scott, Jane. "Buoyant and outrageous, but singer is still fun." *Plain Dealer*. May 6, 1996.

Scott, Jane. "Cars motoring to Coliseum." *Plain Dealer*. October 23, 1987.

Scott, Jane. "Chicago, Beach Boys double date." *Plain Dealer*. April 8, 1988.

Scott, Jane. "Devo: Out of spud fryer into big time." *Plain Dealer*. December 2, 1977.

Scott, Jane. "Did you appreciate?" *Plain Dealer*. August 9, 1968.

Scott, Jane. "Ex-Stones' guitarist gathering no moss." *Plain Dealer*. November 8, 1990.

Scott, Jane. "Fan records Laughner tapes." *Plain Dealer*. July 19, 1982.

Scott, Jane. "Fleetwood Mac leads best of Series." *Plain Dealer*. August 28, 1978.

Scott, Jane. "Getting in and out of Blossom will be easier." *Plain Dealer*. January 14, 1994.

Scott, Jane. "Happy 13th birthday, AC/DC." *Plain Dealer*. 1986.

Scott, Jane. "Here's stars in your eyes." *Plain Dealer*. July 14, 1967.

Scott, Jane "Hot hit star at Front Row ." *Plain Dealer*. September 29, 1989.

Scott, Jane. "Howling from L.A." *Plain Dealer*. February 20, 1987.

Scott, Jane. "Idolizing Public Hall." *Plain Dealer*. March 20, 1987.

Scott, Jane. "Iggy Pop mellows—a little." *Plain Dealer*. March 19, 1994.

Scott, Jane. "Jammin' on string shift." *Plain Dealer*. September 28, 1985.

Scott, Jane. "Jane Scott's 1975 review of the Who concert at Richfield Coliseum." *Plain Dealer*. January 19, 2012.

Scott, Jane. "Jane Scott witness to rock history: A new generation steers rock 'n' roll toward the next millennium." *Plain Dealer*. April 13, 2011.

Scott, Jane. "Jules Belkin: On a roll with Stones and others." *Plain Dealer*. November 17, 1981.

Scott, Jane. "Jimmy Ley not all blues about return." *Plain Dealer*. May 24, 1982.

Scott, Jane. "King, Queen reign at Front Row show." *Plain Dealer*. December 29, 1989.

Scott, Jane. "Maiden metal hits Coliseum." *Plain Dealer*. February 6, 1987.

Scott, Jane. "Marx checks off Coliseum date." *Plain Dealer*. December 15, 1989.

Scott, Jane. "McCartney, Joel concerts here?" *Plain Dealer*. November 24, 1989.

Scott, Jane. "Meat Loaf, Loggins, Southside Johnny due." *Plain Dealer*. August 11, 1978.

Scott, Jane. "Money show is a sure bet." *Plain Dealer*. July 31, 1987.

Scott, Jane. "New wave Phantasy opens tonight." *Plain Dealer*. January 11, 1980.

Scott, Jane. "Newest hot spot is Beachland Ballroom." *Plain Dealer*. March 1, 2000.

Scott, Jane. "No gift of gab in Scot band." *Plain Dealer*. November 17, 1987.

Scott, Jane. "On Beatles, he knows whereof he speaks." *Plain Dealer*. February 9, 1984.

Scott, Jane. "Partnership aims to revive Agora's glory days." *Plain Dealer*. August 29, 1996.

Scott, Jane. "Paul: We put it all in the show." *Plain Dealer*. May 14, 1978.

Scott, Jane. "Pink Floyd voted concert of the year." *Plain Dealer.* February 3, 1978.

Scott, Jane. "Punk Rock: Swastikas and safety pins may be a passport in New York; not here." *Plain Dealer.* July 3, 1977.

Scott, Jane. "Rock turns lights back on in theater." *Plain Dealer.* November 14, 1982.

Scott, Jane. "Rockin' cowboys." *Plain Dealer.* August 1, 1986.

Scott, Jane. "Rolling in Aug. 26 is Fleetwood Mac." *Plain Dealer.* August 6, 1978.

Scott, Jane. "Romantic rock." Plain Dealer. October 25, 1981.

Scott, Jane. "Rush back on favorite turf." *Plain Dealer.* November 13, 1987.

Scott, Jane. "Sample a taste of Jamaica." *Plain Dealer.* December 19, 1986.

Scott, Jane. "Stevie Wonder rocks Coliseum." *Plain Dealer.* October 29, 1987.

Scott, Jane. "Sounds of Who are still Entwistle." *Plain Dealer.* June 17, 1988.

Scott, Jane. "'Spring Jam' means hot soul." *Plain Dealer.* March 31, 1989.

Scott, Jane. "Springsteen pulls out all the stops." *Plain Dealer.* July 31, 1981.

Scott, Jane. "Star-studded Series kicks off with improvements." *Plain Dealer.* July 11, 1980.

Scott, Jane. "Still surprising after all this time." *Plain Dealer.* April 1, 1996.

Scott, Jane. "Stones hope to return in 1983." *Plain Dealer.* November 20, 1981.

Scott, Jane. "'Stones' Mobbed as Concert Ends." *Plain Dealer.* June 16, 1966.

Scott, Jane. "Strut set for Lakewood." *Plain Dealer.* October 15, 1976.

Scott, Jane. "Thank you, too." *Plain Dealer.* July 26, 1968.

Scott, Jane. "The Doors, Morrison Light Their Fires." *Plain Dealer.* August 4, 1968.

Scott, Jane. "The Happening." *Plain Dealer.* August 16, 1974.

Scott, Jane. "The Happening." *Plain Dealer.* October 3, 1969.

Scott, Jane. "The Happening." *Plain Dealer.* October 18, 1974.

Scott, Jane. "The sweet squish of success." *Plain Dealer.* July 18, 1986.

Scott, Jane. "There's room for punk in rock museum." *Plain Dealer.* November 25, 1994.

Scott, Jane. "Tour brings Clapton to Cleveland in April." *Plain Dealer.* February 20, 1998.

Scott, Jane. "Veteran punk group still is wowing crowds here the Ramones." *Plain Dealer.* October 16, 1991.

Scott, Jane. "WHO Concert Is Screaming Success." *Plain Dealer.* July 15, 1968.

Scott, Jane. "Who's music is all right." *Plain Dealer.* December 7, 1979.

Scott, Jane. "Willio and Phillio: Humor and harmony." *Plain Dealer.* March 17, 1978.

Scott, Jane. "Young Folks Take Trip at Musicarnival." *Plain Dealer.* July 21, 1969.

Scott, Jane. "Zeppelin goes over big." *Plain Dealer.* April 29, 1977.

Singleton, Tyler. "For Sale: A Slice of Cleveland Music History." *Scene.* July 17, 2015.

Soeder, John. "65 high school bands graduate to Odeon stage." *Plain Dealer.* January 1, 1999.

Soeder, John. "A local legend gets a leg up." *Plain Dealer.* May 21, 2002.

Soeder, John. "Music club's forecast good. Many hope Beachland is the start of sunnier days for the Waterloo Rd. business district." *Plain Dealer.* November 9, 2000.

Soeder, John. "Odeon Concert Club in Flats to close March 1. Owner cites local economy , competition from House of Blues." *Plain Dealer*. December 14, 2005.

Soeder, John. "Peabody's relocating ; Dance club set to open." *Plain Dealer*. June 21, 2000.

Soeder, John. "Rock still beating a path to the door, Venerable venue turns 40 years old." *Plain Dealer*. February 26, 2006.

Thoma, Pauline. "Homestead Theater may become a mall." *Plain Dealer*. November 2, 1979.

Tomazic, Mary Ellen. "Cleveland's Underground Music Scene, 1967–1979." *Negative Print Fanzine*. September 1983

Warner, Susan E. & Jayne A. Thompson. "1 killed, many hurt as violence mars concert at Stadium." *Plain Dealer*. July 29, 1979.

Weigel, Tom. "It's all clear for the Pirate's Cove." *Plain Dealer*. August 21, 1970.

Williams, Valena Minor. "Call & Post Woman's Editor Caught in Wild Melee as: Moon Doggers 'Break it Up'." *Call & Post*. March 29, 1952.

Wolff, Carlo. "Musicians poised to become stars." *Plain Dealer*. July 26, 1996.

Wolff, Carlo. "Phantasy under siege by fans in a frenzy." *Plain Dealer*. June 13, 1987.

Wolff, Carlo. "Veteran hip-hop group disses eager fans." *Plain Dealer*. March 16, 1999.

Wooten, Dick, "22,000 scream for McCartney." *Cleveland Press*. May 11, 1976.

Yarborough, Chuck. "Roast, toast and concert pay homage to Agora founder Hank LoConti Sr." *Plain Dealer*. March 22, 2013.

Yarborough, Chuck. "Winchester owner Jim Mileti closes doors on club, wants 'to do what's right in the Lord'." *Plain Dealer*. May 13, 2014.

OTHER BOOKS OF INTEREST . . .

Cleveland Radio Tales
Stories from the Local Radio Scene of the 1960s, '70s, '80s, and '90s

Mike Olszewski, Janice Olszewski

Remember when Cleveland radio crackled with larger-than-life characters? Meet dozens of intriguing personalities like "Count" John Manolesco, the talk show host and former vampire who performed an exorcism live on-air, a daytime jock who once did his show in the nude, teenage "pirate" radio operators, unruly studio guests, and many more true tales.

Cleveland Rock & Roll Memories
True and Tall Tales of the Glory Days, Told by Musicians, DJs, Promoters, and Fans Who Made the Scene in the '60s, '70s, and '80s

Carlo Wolff

Clevelanders who grew up with Rock and Roll in the 1960s, '70s, and '80s remember a golden age, with clubs like the Agora, trendsetting radio stations WIXY 1260 and WMMS, Coffee Break Concerts, The World Series of Rock. Includes first-person stories by fans, musicians, DJs, reporters, club owners, and more, with rare photos and memorabilia.

Cleveland TV Tales
Stories from the Golden Age of Local Television

Mike Olszewski, Janice Olszewski

Remember when TV was just three channels and the biggest celebrities in Cleveland were a movie host named Ghoulardi, an elf named Barnaby, and a newscaster named Dorothy Fuldheim? Revisit the early days in these lively stories about the pioneering entertainers who invented television programming before our very eyes. Filled with fun details.

More at **www.grayco.com**

OTHER BOOKS OF INTEREST . . .

Cleveland TV Tales Volume 2
More Stories from the Golden Age of Local Television

Mike Olszewski, Janice Olszewski

More behind-the-screen stories from Cleveland TV history (1960s-'90s), including the rise of glamorous news anchors with big hair and perky noses, battling horror-movie hosts, investigative reporters stalking wrongdoers on both sides of the law, a daytime host's bizarre scandal, a mayor who co-hosted with a ventriloquist's dummy, and much more.

The Buzzard
Inside the Glory Days of WMMS and Cleveland Rock Radio—A Memoir

John Gorman, Tom Feran

This rock and roll radio memoir goes behind the scenes at the nation's hottest station during FM's heyday, from 1973 to 1986. It was a wild and creative time. John Gorman and a small band of true believers remade rock radio while Cleveland staked its claim as the "Rock and Roll Capital." Filled with juicy insider details.

"Gorman describes in exclusive, behind-the-scenes detail the state of rock 'n' roll from the early '70s to the late '80s, when just about anything happened and everyone looked the other way . . . Essential reading for musicians, entertainment industry leaders, and music fans." – Mike Shea, CEO/Co-Founder, Alternative Press magazine

Cleveland Summertime Memories
A Warm Look Back

Gail Ghetia Bellamy

What made the summertime special to a Cleveland kid? Building sandcastles in your clam diggers at Edgewater Park. Pulling up to Manners Big Boy in your parents' car for a burger and a Big Ghoulardi. An ornate sundae at Boukair's. Watching the Indians lose (again) at Municipal Stadium. Being terrified by Laughing Sal at Euclid Beach Park. And more!Includes first-person stories by fans, musicians, DJs, reporters, club owners, and more, with rare photos and memorabilia.

More at **www.grayco.com**